Grammar Contexts

Grammar Contexts

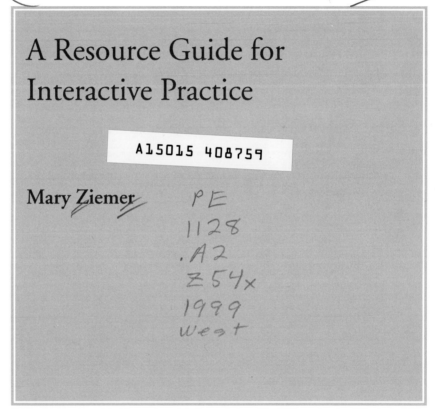

A Resource Guide for Interactive Practice

Mary Ziemer

Ann Arbor
THE UNIVERSITY OF MICHIGAN PRESS

To my teachers and my students

Preface

When teaching grammar to beginning, intermediate, and advanced students in Intensive English Programs at the high school and college levels, I have been grateful that the textbooks provided clear rules, multiple examples, and plenty of practice exercises that helped the students to focus on a given grammatical structure. Although the textbooks were useful as a teaching tool, I often felt frustrated because the grammar exercises felt unreal and disconnected from everyday life and language usage, and, although my students were adept at filling in the blanks found in their textbooks, it often seemed that they could not transfer their knowledge of grammatical structures used in isolated exercises to oral and written production. When they had to deal with content-based materials, the students seemed unable to apply the grammar rules they had learned in class. So, I felt that the students needed more opportunities to practice grammatical structures that were related to a particular context, whether that context be a song, speech, poem, cartoon or a line from a play—as long as the material provided the basis for social interaction and contextualized the practice of a grammatical form.

I also found that while the predictable structure of the textbooks made teaching easier for me—and the classroom experience more secure for my students—lessons based upon the textbook activities often became mechanical and flat. What I needed was a way to use the text as a jumping off point for the creation of more contextualized activities that would help the students make the move from simply understanding a grammar rule to actually applying the rule in a more natural way.

When I looked to grammar resource books for ideas, I found many good examples of creative games and "fillers" but few suggestions for how I could more fully contextualize a grammatical structure to make it more real and meaningful for the students. And, while I had plenty of communicative activities to choose from, I still had to spend time trying to extend them into a more integrated lesson plan that not only brought together the skills of listening, speaking, reading, and writing but also provided the framework for a contextualized understanding of grammar points. *Grammar Contexts: A Resource Guide for Interactive Practice* came together as I tried to find topic-centered tasks that could be used to enliven one-dimensional grammar exercises for my intermediate students and their teacher.

To make this resource book easier for teachers to use, I have provided a User's Guide that more fully explains the purpose of the resource book, the terminology used in the materials, and the overall organization of the text and activities.

As instructors will see, I have tried to include a wide variety of activities in this resource book. Bringing grammatical forms to life is an experience in the dynamic nature of communication and a creative experience that requires support from other ESL/EFL instructors. A number of the ideas that I have come up with are adaptations and extensions of activities that were inspired by other instructors, and I have attempted to acknowledge such sources of inspiration whenever this was possible.

I would like to acknowledge the following people for having provided the original form of a particular activity.

1.1.   Winn-Bell Olsen. From a study (1980) cited in *The Grammar Book: An ESL/EFL Teacher's Course* by Marianne Celce-Murcia and Diane Larsen-Freeman (Boston: Heinle & Heinle Publishers, 1983), 115.

2.3.   Natalie Pret, Intensive English Program, University of Washington, Grammar 3 (1995).

2.6.   Elaine Kirn and Pamela Hartmann, eds., *Interactions II: A Reading Skills Book* (New York: McGraw-Hill Companies, 1996), 85–89.

2.7.   Richard Moore, Intensive English Program, University of Washington, Grammar 3 (1995).

2.9.   Timothy Eyres. An adaptation of unpublished teacher training materials presented at the Teacher's Training College, Torun, Poland (1991–92).

3.7.   Kay Landolt, Intensive English Program, University of Washington, Grammar 3 (1995).

3.9.   Marianne Celce-Murcia and Diane Larsen-Freeman, for a lesson based on a suggestion made in *The Grammar Book: An ESL/EFL Teacher's Course* (Boston: Heinle & Heinle Publishers, 1983), 119.

4.2.   Natalie Pret, Intensive English Program, University of Washington, Grammar 3 (1995).

4.3.   Timothy Eyres. An adaptation of unpublished teacher training materials presented at the Teacher's Training College, Torun, Poland (1991–92). And also Penny Ur from her *Grammar Practice Activities: A Practical Guide for Teachers* (Cambridge: Cambridge University Press, 1988), 245.

4.4.   Ellen Kohn. United States Peace Corps, Technical Coordinating Supervisor. Latvia (1993).

4.5.   Dr. Heidi Riggenbach, University of Washington, MATESOL program, English 575 (1995).

4.8.   Timothy Eyres. An adaptation of teacher training materials presented at the Teacher's Training College, Torun, Poland (1991–92).

4.8.   Dr. Sandra Silberstein. An adaptation of an activity in *Techniques and Resources in Teaching Reading* (Oxford: Oxford University Press, 1994), 4–5.

5.3.   Betsy Branch. An adaptation of an activity in *The Grammar Book: An ESL/EFL Teacher's Course* by Marianne Celce-Murcia and Diane Larsen-Freeman (Boston: Heinle & Heinle Publishers, 1983), 89. Unpublished course project, English 575, University of Washington, MATESOL program (1995).

5.4.   Betsy Branch. An adaptation of an activity in *The Grammar Book: An ESL/EFL Teacher's Course* by Marianne Celce-Murcia and Diane Larsen-Freeman (Boston: Heinle & Heinle Publishers, 1983), 89. Unpublished course project, English 575, University of Washington, MATESOL program (1995).

5.7.   Betsy Branch. Unpublished course project, English 575, University of Washington, MATESOL program (1995).

5.11. Debra Folden and Jacqueline Fisher. Unpublished course project, English 575, University of Washington, MATESOL program (1995).

8.4.   Zeinab El-Naggar. An adaptation of an activity in *The Grammar Book: An ESL/EFL Teacher's Course* by Marianne Celce-Murcia and Diane Larsen-Freeman (Boston: Heinle & Heinle Publishers, 1983), 320.

8.6.   Timothy Eyres. An adaptation of unpublished teacher training materials presented at the Teacher's Training College, Torun, Poland (1991–92).

I am also gratefully indebted to Michael Swan for a lecture he gave at the 1997 annual meeting for the English Teachers Association of Switzerland entitled "What Makes a Good Rule?" and to the example of clear and simple grammar rules that he has provided in his book *How English Works: A Grammar Practice Book* (Oxford: Oxford University Press, 1997) that he co-authored with Catherine Walter.

I would also like to formally acknowledge my trainers for the United States Peace Corps in Poland (1990) especially Joan Borsvold, Brenda Bowman, Dr. Mary Schleppegrell, and Dr. Jean Zukowski/Faust. Special thanks are due to Timothy Eyres, a colleague of mine at the Teacher's Training College in Torun, Poland, who so generously shared with me his expertise as a trainer for British certification in Teaching English as a Foreign Language, and to Natalie Pret, my mentor when I taught grammar in the University of

Washington's Intensive English Program. Also, while working on these materials, I have greatly appreciated the suggestions and optimism provided by Sylvia Nadig, my friend and colleague, and by Bill Harshbarger, my director in the Intensive English Program at the University of Washington.

I am extremely grateful to Dr. Heidi Riggenbach of the University of Washington, who first encouraged me to write this resource book and who then gave me her valuable guidance as I prepared the manuscript.

Finally, I would like to thank the University of Michigan Press for their confidence in this work and Kelly Sippell, Editor for ESL Acquisitions, for her unfailing patience and support.

Acknowledgments

To those who have granted permission to use copyrighted material, I offer this grateful acknowledgment.

Harburg, E. Y., and Arlen, Harold. "If I Only Had a Brain/Heart/Nerve," © 1938 (Renewed) by Metro-Goldwyn-Mayer Inc. © 1939 (Renewed) by EMI Feist Catalog Inc. Reprinted by permission of Warner Bros. Publications, A Warner Music Group Company.

Henry Holt and Company, Inc., for "The Road Not Taken," by Robert Frost. From *The Poetry of Robert Frost* edited by Edward Connery Lathem, Copyright © 1944 by Robert Frost. Copyright 1916, © 1969 by Henry Holt and Company, Inc. Reprinted by permission of Henry Holt and Company, Inc.

McGraw-Hill, for an illustration from "Lifestyles," in *Interactions II: A Reading Skills Book,* 3rd edition, edited by Elaine Kirn and Pamela Hartmann, Copyright © 1996, 1990, 1985. Reprinted by permission of The McGraw-Hill Companies.

New Directions Publishing Company for "This is Just to Say," by William Carlos Williams, from *The Collected Poems, 1909–1939, Vol. I.* Copyright © 1938 by New Directions Publishing Corporation. Reprinted by permission of New Directions Publishing Corporation.

Random House, Inc., for excerpt from *Happy Birthday to You!* by Dr. Seuss™, copyright © 1959 and renewed 1987 by Dr. Seuss Enterprises, L. P. Reprinted by permission of Random House, Inc., and International Creative Management, Inc. All rights reserved.

Satyamurti, Carole. "I Shall Paint My Nails Red." From *Changing the Subject* by Carole Satyamurti. Copyright © Carole Satyamurti 1990; reprinted from *Changing the Subject* by Carole Satyamurti (1990) by permission of Oxford University Press.

Universal Press Syndicate for a "Dear Abby" column by Abigail Van Buren. "Non-Russian-Speaking Wife Feels She's Left Out." Copyright © 1995 Universal Press Syndicate. Reprinted with permission. All rights reserved.

Warner Bros. Publications, Inc., for "Let's Call the Whole Thing Off," Music and Lyrics by GEORGE GERSHWIN and IRA GERSHWIN. © 1936, 1937 GEORGE GERSHWIN MUSIC and IRA GERSHWIN MUSIC. Copyrights Renewed/All Rights Administered by WB MUSIC CORP. Gershwin®, George Gershwin® and Ira Gershwin™ are trademarks of Gershwin Enterprises. Used by Permission of the Publishers and Warner Bros. Publications U.S. Inc. All Rights Reserved.

The scripture quotations from Ecclesiastes 3:1–8 and I Corinthians 13:1–7 contained herein have been adapted from the *New Standard Version Bible.* Copyright © 1989 by the Division of Christian Education of the National Council of the Churches of Christ in the U.S.A. Used by permission. All rights reserved.

Contents

Introduction: User's Guide

What Is the Purpose of This Resource Book?

This resource book is entitled *Grammar Contexts: A Resource Guide for Interactive Practice* because the activities and lesson plans are meant to connect isolated grammar textbook exercises to situations and topics that occur in real life. Context-rich topics and tasks are interwoven with the use of grammatical structures to help make the meaning and usage of a particular form clearer to intermediate-level students at the high school and college levels. The activities in this book are also meant to provide teachers with fresh ideas to enhance textbook materials that may have become unexciting through repetitive use.

Many times, ESL/EFL instructors may want to more fully contextualize a grammar point but are hesitant to do so because of questions such as the following.

- What if the content I've chosen to work with confuses my students?
- What if my students don't know the vocabulary needed to understand a topic?
- Am I teaching grammar or culture?
- Will my students be prepared for grammar tests if I focus on context in class?
- Where will I find the time to include contextualized activities and complete the exercises in the textbook?

The aim of this resource book is simply to provide activities and lessons that may help resolve some of the issues raised by these questions. Often, when a grammar point is studied through the use of contextualized materials, the students are overwhelmed by new vocabulary and ideas that distract them from the understanding and application of a grammar rule. The activities and lessons in this resource book are intended to remedy this problem by making context-based materials more readily accessible as a vehicle for language study.

As a rule, the resource materials in this book build upon the foundation that has already been provided by the clear analysis of grammar rules and the multiple practice exercises found in grammar textbooks. While grammar textbook exercises help students to master the form of a grammatical structure through the use of isolated or discrete-item exercises, the activities in this resource book help students to apply grammatical forms when they are used in everyday life by developing topic-centered tasks that create a context for more lifelike communication.

In this particular resource book, I have chosen to include the forms that my intermediate students have been required to review or to learn and that they have found difficult to conceptualize in terms of meaning and usage.

The Present Tense
The Past Tense
The Future Tense
The Present Perfect
Modal Auxiliary Verbs
Gerunds and Infinitives
Conditionals: Using *If* to Express Unreal Past Situations and Using *Wish*
Connecting Words

For practical purposes, I have also chosen to limit the number of structures covered so that the resource book would not become too large and unwieldy for instructors to use. In the future, I hope to prepare similar resource materials for other structures that intermediate students often deal with, in particular, articles, adverbs, nouns, pronouns, prepositions, adjective clauses, the comparison of adjectives, the passive voice, and interrogatives. However, to retain the fully developed nature of the materials in this resource book, I have had to limit the number of structures included in the text.

To save teachers preparation time, the directions for all the activities are written in a step-by-step fashion and are often accompanied by ready-made resource materials. The directions are there to serve as a model and as a support, not as the definitive format for an activity, so instructors should freely adapt the directions to their own teaching style and/or to the personality of a particular class. Experienced teachers are invited to scan over what seems self-evident to them. Novice teachers are invited to read the directions with more care.

Instructors should feel free to pick and choose from the activities found in this resource book since there are more than could possibly be used in a quarter or semester and some activities will suit the level, personality, and purpose of a given class better than others. Likewise, some lessons may suit a given instructor better than others. In this resource book, I have included a wide variety of materials to appeal to various learning styles and intelligences; for instance, I have provided activities for those students who learn best through the use of problem-solving and charts, visual activities, kinesthetic activities, and/or music and song. Additionally, I have varied the group work to appeal to those students who favor individual work, or intrapersonal activities, such as journal and poetry writing, and those who favor group work, or interpersonal activities, such as information gap activities and role plays. Here I would like to encourage instructors who generally shy away from using poetry or song in favor of more "functional" language to consider using the poems and lyrics noted in these materials. To this end, I would argue that language itself is metaphorical and that the study of poetic or lyrical language also serves a useful function for ESL/EFL students: it helps to make them more aware of the rhetorical effects possible through a metaphoric and rhythmic use of the English language.

In this resource book, I have sought to include thought-provoking activities and lessons that allow for critical thinking, creativity, and meaningful discussions. Whenever possible, I have encouraged instructors to include culturally relevant models for their students and to be sensitive to cross-cultural perspectives. I would also ask that instructors be culturally sensitive when selecting an activity or a lesson that may be in conflict with the political, social, and/or religious mores of the country in which they are teaching or of individual students in a given class.

To personalize this advice, I would like to share my experience in the United States Peace Corps. At our training, we were told of a Peace Corps volunteer who used materials which were interpreted as being critical of a country's government. As a result, the Peace Corps was asked to leave that country. On the more positive side, when I was a teacher trainer in Poland, I was impressed when some of my students chose to use Dr. Martin Luther King, Jr.'s principles of nonviolent direct action to protest school administrative policies that they felt were unfair. In both examples, materials used in the classroom had life-changing effects on the students as well as their communities.

To aid instructors in the development of culturally relevant materials, I have included a number of activities and lessons that relate to the lives of well-known cultural figures—both living and historical. When using such materials in class, an instructor cannot assume that all his or her students are familiar with the same well-known individuals. In my own experience as a student of German, I recall an instructor who was obviously disappointed when only one student out of fourteen knew anything about the life of the eighteenth-century German writer Johann Wolfgang von Goethe. I wondered if the instructor could have, in turn, mentioned the names of well-known poets from other countries. So, in order to avoid similar situations and to help instructors create a language-learning community with a shared body of cultural knowledge, I suggest that early on in a class instructors use activities that introduce the lives of such people to their students. Once the students are familiar with the vocabulary and cultural information associated with the lives of given individuals, then these people's lives can be used as a means of contextualizing grammar practice activities. In this way, the recycled context can be used as a vehicle for language practice without causing the students to be distracted by new vocabulary terms and socio-cultural information.

For this reason, many of the materials in this resource book use the lives and/or life works of well-known cultural figures to contextualize the use of a grammatical structure—in particular, activities 1.2, 1.3, 2.2, 3.2, 4.1, 6.2, 7.2, and extended lessons 3.10, 3.11, 4.8, and 7.6. I recommend that instructors familiarize themselves with these activities and lessons so that they will have an idea of how such materials are used to integrate the lives of well-known people with the practice of a grammatical structure.

Among the people referred to in this resource book, instructors will find artists, composers, musicians, poets, novelists, playwrights, politicians, scientists, actors, sports figures, mystics, and religious leaders. In general, such cultural figures are from English-speaking or European countries; however, in the directions to activities and lessons, I encourage instructors to have their students apply the format of a given exercise to the lives of cultural figures from their own national heritage. Among the people referred to in these materials, instructors will find the following individuals.

Vincent van Gogh	Bill Gates	The President of the United States
John Lennon	Elizabeth Taylor	Frédéric Chopin
Kaga no Chiyo	Marilyn Monroe	Emily Dickinson
Robert Frost	William Shakespeare	Ernest Hemingway
Michael Jordan	The Princess of Wales	Dr. Martin Luther King, Jr.
Margaret Thatcher	Mother Teresa	Paul McCartney
St. Francis of Assisi	William Blake	Wolfgang Amadeus Mozart
Paul of Tarsus	Nicholas Copernicus	Alfred, Lord Tennyson
Alice Walker	Maurice Wilkins	Galileo
Helen Keller	L. Frank Baum	James Watson
Abraham Lincoln	Nostradamus	Theodor Seuss Geisel (Dr. Seuss)
Christina Rossetti		James Stephens

(Biographical information on hundreds of well-known figures can be accessed on the Internet via www.biography.com.) When students use contexts related to the lives of these and other cultural figures, they learn not only about language use but also about life.

Itemized Reference Lists

An itemized list of the activities in a chapter is intended to make it easier for instructors to find the type of activity they would like to use. The reference list indicates the skills used in the activity—listening, speaking, reading, and/

or writing—and the means of learning, for example, problem solving, personalization, information gap, dialogues, songs, and poetry. The reference list also indicates whether an activity requires individual, pair, and/or small group work or work by the class as a whole. Instructors should feel free, however, to select the type of group work they'd like to use for a given activity or stage in a lesson. Additionally, the reference list identifies which activities are accompanied by ready-made resource materials.

Chapter Organization

In each chapter, the activities for particular grammatical structures are divided into two sections: supplementary activities, which generally take from ten to twenty minutes to complete, and extended lesson plans, which give instructors the option of more fully developing a context for the practice of a grammar point. In general, extended lessons require a fifty-minute class session to complete, allowing for time to take attendance, etc. Both the supplementary activities and extended lesson plans are geared toward intermediate and/or high-intermediate students of English grammar. Even so, many of the activities can also be used with more advanced learners and in other skill-based courses. Additionally, the approach used to organize activities and lessons can readily be adapted to developing materials for beginning-level students.

Supplementary Activities

The supplementary activities provide short, contextualized tasks for the practice of grammatical structures that have previously been introduced in class. A context may be built around a famous quotation, a picture, a role play, or a time line. Since most of the supplementary activities are meant to take from ten to twenty minutes to complete, I have not suggested an exact time frame for the completion of each supplementary activity; instead, I have left this to the instructor, who can better judge how much time is required given the classroom dynamics and time constraints. I have expanded a number of supplementary activities into extended lessons and instructors may decide to do likewise with some of the other supplementary activities.

Extended Lesson Plans

The extended lessons more fully develop a context for the study and practice of a grammar point. These lessons also give learners the opportunity to apply their knowledge of a grammatical structure. Both the extended lesson plans and the supplementary activities generally follow three stages of development.

1. Presentation
2. Practice
3. Application

However, since the supplementary lessons are less developed than the extended lessons, I have delineated these stages only as they apply to the extended lessons. For the extended lessons, I have suggested time frames for each of the three stages of the lesson so that the entire lesson can be completed in approximately forty-five minutes. Instructors should note that a lesson need not necessarily be completed in one day. When teaching many of these lessons myself, I have sometimes chosen to expand or contract them, depending on the objectives my students and I sought to achieve and on the amount of time we had. To save time in class, instructors may also choose to have students work on a portion of a lesson for homework rather than as classwork. Also, an instructor might decide to save one stage of the lesson for the next day as a way to break up the usual class routine.

1. Presentation

   This portion of the lesson serves as a preview of the material found in the context and as a warm-up to spark the students' interest in the lesson. The presentation may also review a grammatical form with which the students should be familiar in order to fully participate in the subsequent stages of the lesson. Generally, new vocabulary related to the content of a lesson is also introduced at this stage. In essence, the presentation stage gives instructors the opportunity to preteach what the students need to know before they can successfully apply their knowledge of a grammatical form to how the form is actually used in a given context.

2. Practice

   At this point in the lesson, students are given the opportunity to practice using the material that has been reviewed or pretaught in the presentation. The majority of the activities in the practice stage are of a controlled nature and require students to work in pairs or small groups. During group work, instructors have the opportunity to provide their students with individual feedback. Also, the activities give instructors the chance to assess their students' comprehension of the material before they are asked to apply their knowledge in a more open-ended activity.

3. Application
   During the final stage of the lesson, students are given the opportunity to use a structure creatively in a "real-life" application. This application allows for more natural communication than in the practice stage, and the tasks are generally more open-ended. In this stage, the students typically generate their own content based on the framework established during the presentation and practice stages of the lesson. To shorten an extended lesson, instructors might be tempted to leave off the application stage, but I would suggest that they leave time for this stage whenever possible: students rarely have the opportunity to creatively apply the grammatical structures they have learned in class, and it is this stage in particular that makes a grammatical form applicable to the students' lives.

Resource Materials

In the Appendixes found at the end of each chapter, instructors will find ready-made resource materials for a given activity. These resource materials are meant to make the preparation time shorter for instructors and to serve as models for additional materials that can be made for an activity. Resource materials that are marked © 1998 University of Michigan may be photocopied. Materials that are marked *public domain* may be copied as they are no longer under copyright obligations. All other materials require permission from the copyright holder to photocopy those materials for distribution. Copyrights are noted on the resource materials. (Please note that copyrighted song lyrics, poems, and texts that are found on the Internet also require permission from the copyright holder for classroom distribution.)

To avoid copyright problems, I generally suggest that an instructor write the copyrighted materials on the board, on an overhead transparency, or on flip chart paper, rather than photocopying the copyrighted materials. For this reason, I have tried to select works that are relatively short. Instructors will find suggestions for dealing with copyrighted materials in the directions for a given activity or lesson plan.

Bibliography

The activities in this book are meant to build on the grammar rules and structures that have already been discussed in a grammar class. Because of this rationale, the bibliography provides instructors with suggested titles for grammar reference books. And, since I do not always give ideas for teaching and/or eliciting vocabulary words, I have also included titles of reference books for the teaching of vocabulary. Additionally, the bibliography supplies instructors with the titles of other grammar resource books.

The Web of Life

I hope that instructors find using this resource book a positive experience. I would welcome feedback about the experiences instructors have had using these materials. I would also welcome additional suggestions for activities related to the structures presented in this book. If you would like to share your experiences and ideas with me, please access the Web site for this resource book on the Internet *Grammar Contexts* at the University of Michigan Press ESL Web site at: www.press.umich.edu/esl/.

As mentioned previously, I have not included chapters related to the contextualized teaching of grammatical structures such as articles, adverbs, nouns, pronouns, prepositions, adjective clauses, the comparison of adjectives, the passive voice, and interrogatives. However, I would very much like to compile both supplementary and extended lessons for these and other structures. If you have ideas for such contextualized lessons, please add your suggestions to the database found on the Web site. Should I use your idea(s) in a future publication, the reference will be fully cited.

As language teachers become familiar with the approach I have taken to the development of a more meaningful context for grammar practice activities, it is my hope that they, in turn, will apply similar strategies in their own lessons. No doubt, there are many ESL/EFL teachers who have already applied similar teaching techniques—I hope to hear from you soon!

Thank you again to those noted in the preface who have already contributed to this book, and thank you in advance for your contributions to a future resource book. I'm glad that you've looked into *Grammar Contexts: A Resource Guide for Interactive Practice,* and I hope it proves to be a useful and enjoyable teaching tool.

Chapter 1
The Present Tense

Itemized Reference List

Skill Areas		Group Work	
Listening	L	Individual	i
Speaking	S	Pair	ii
Reading	R	Small Group	iii+
Writing	W	Class	iiiii

Structure		Activity	Skills	Groups	Appendix
Supplementary Activities					
1.1.	Answering *Yes/No* Questions	Role play	L, S	ii & iiiii	33
1.2.	Frequency Adverbs and *How Often . . . ?*	Biography	L, S, W	i & ii	
1.3.	Nonprogressive Verbs	Second identity	L, S	ii	34
1.4.	Nonprogressive Verbs	Visual focus	L, S	ii	36
1.5.	Progressive and Nonprogressive Verbs	Visual focus	L, S, W	ii & iiiii	37
1.6.	Progressive Verbs and Using *Probably*	Time zones	L, S	ii & iiiii	38
1.7.	The Simple Present and Present Progressive	Autobiography	L, S, W	i & iiiii	
Extended Lessons					
1.8.	The Simple Present and Time Clauses: Poem				
1.8a.	Presentation	Sentence completion	L, S, W	ii & iiiii	39
1.8b.	Practice	Sequencing	R	ii & iiiii	41
1.8c.	Application	Time clauses	W	i & iii+	42
1.9.	The Simple Present and Present Progressive: Haiku				
1.9a.	Presentation and Practice	Questions and answers	L, S, R	ii & iiiii	
1.9b.	Application	Writing haiku	W	i & ii & iii+ & iiiii	
1.10.	The Simple Present: Poem				
1.10a.	Presentation	Word association	L, S	i & ii & iiiii	44
1.10b.	Practice	Discourse analysis	L, S, R	i & ii & iiiii	45
1.10c.	Application	Creature poem	W	i	
1.11.	The Present Tense: Definition				
1.11a.	Presentation	Definition	L, S, W	i & ii & iiiii	
1.11b.	Practice: Option One	Cloze	L, S, R	i & ii & iiiii	46
1.11b.	Practice: Option Two	Parallelism	R, W	i & ii & iiiii	47
1.11c.	Application	Definition	L, S, W	i & iiiii	48

Supplementary Activities

1.1. Answering *Yes/No* Questions

> **Role play; L, S; ii & iiiii**
> **Materials included**

Often, exercises that list responses to *yes/no* questions use a mechanical format in which students are to respond by saying, "Yes she or he does" or "No she or he doesn't," to the appropriate prompt. However, students may be interested to know that native speakers rarely answer direct questions with such short forms and that when they do, the answer can sound very abrupt and can have a negative connotation, especially in formal situations.

Winn-Bell Olsen (1980) conducted a study in which she found that 92 percent of the time, native speakers responded to *yes/no* questions with reduced or informal forms of *yes* such as *yep, yeah, uh-huh* or of *no* such as *nah, nope,* or *uh-uh*. Also, native speakers occasionally answered questions indirectly, saying, for example, "I doubt it," if they were not sure of the appropriate answer.

Although students may require knowledge of the formal response for exams it would be a worthwhile exercise to explore more natural responses that students have heard. With the students, brainstorm other possible responses such as *probably, most likely, maybe, I think so, totally,* etc., and have them use these forms and the reduced informal forms when answering the *yes/no* questions found in a textbook. This is a good time to point out the social context in which a particular response is generally used.

Also, you can point out that people often answer a *yes/no* question by simply responding with a related statement but not necessarily with a *yes* or *no*. For example, a person might answer the question, "Do you think it will rain today?" by saying, "Well, it rained yesterday," leaving it to the listener to make a logical conclusion based on the response.

To provide students with the opportunity to practice the various responses to *yes/no* questions, give pairs of students a slip of paper on which you have written a particular situation. (There is a list of possible situations in Appendix 1.1.) Ask the students to think of *yes/no* questions they might ask to get more information about this situation. For example, consider the questions a person renting a new apartment might have.

- Does it have a view?
- Is it expensive?
- Is there a store nearby?

- Are the neighbors quiet?
- Are there laundry facilities?
- Is parking available?

In pairs, one student can ask the questions and the other can respond using the various forms discussed in class. You may need to preteach some of the vocabulary involved. You may also have to adjust some of the situations to the cultural context in which you find yourself teaching. If there is time, have pairs role-play their respective situations for the class and ask the other students to guess what the situation is. Encourage the students to come up with possible responses that are not necessarily *yes* or *no.* For example, to the question, "Does it have a view?" the landlord might answer, "You can see a bit of the lake from here" or "There's an apartment building across the street." If your students are familiar with the use of past and future tenses, encourage them to use these forms in their questions as well.

1.2. Frequency Adverbs and *How Often . . . ?*

Biography; L, S, W; i & ii

To liven up activities based on frequency adverbs such as *always, usually, often, sometimes, seldom, rarely,* and *never,* you can have students apply these adverbs to the actions of famous people. With your students, brainstorm a list of well-known people, living or dead, with whom the students are familiar. (See the User's Guide for more on using the lives of well-known people to contextualize grammatical structures.) Then prepare the students to use frequency adverbs in a verbal description of what each person on the list does in his or her life.

As an example, elicit information about Bill Gates (William Henry Gates III, 1955–), by asking a series of who-what-when-where-why questions such as

1. Who is Bill Gates? (The chairman and chief executive officer of Microsoft Corporation)
2. What is he known for? (Developing programming languages for personal computers, computer software, and computer operating systems)
3. When do you use his products? (When you use Microsoft products)
4. Where is Microsoft's main headquarters? (In Seattle, Washington)
5. Why is Gates so famous? (Because he developed a technology that

is used by so many people and because he is one of the richest individuals in the world. Also, some people have accused him of trying
to monopolize the software industry.)

Based on the answers to these questions, the students might come up
with the following activities and frequency adverbs that could be associated
with the life of Bill Gates.

Bill Gates *usually* gets up early and stays up late. He *often* works on computers. He *seldom* leaves the office. He's *never* without a good idea for
computer software. *Sometimes,* he donates money to schools.

In the case of a person who is no longer living, students will need to
speak as if a person were still alive in order to practice the present tense;
however, if your students are already able to use the past tense, then you can
encourage them to use this form as well. In the case of the Dutch painter
Vincent van Gogh (1853–90), a student might say:

Vincent van Gogh *usually* paints every day. He *often* paints into the night.
He *rarely* has money. *Sometimes* he paints stars or sunflowers.

It is interesting to have the students present information about famous
people from their own countries. As a follow-up activity, you can have pairs
of students role-play an interview in which one student takes on the persona
of the individual whose life she or he had described and another student
role-plays a journalist who asks questions using frequency adverbs such as,
"What do you usually do?" etc. You can also have students practice asking,
"How often do you . . . ?" during the interviews. Remind the students to use
the first-person point of view when responding to the questions. Encourage
them to add questions that do not necessarily include frequency adverbs.

If you would like to incorporate the skill of writing, you can expand the
activity by having the students write a biographical sketch about the person
they have already discussed. Students can simply write out what they have
already said about a person and add other descriptive sentences. So, for van
Gogh, a student might write something a bit more elaborate such as

He usually paints every day in the fields. He often likes to paint sunflowers
that look like a fire. Sometimes he paints at night because he likes to
paint the stars. He rarely sees his brother Theo, so he often writes him
letters. Sometimes he borrows money from Theo.

You can then collect these biographical sketches and compile them into a work entitled *The Lives of Famous People* so that the students can read one another's biographies. If you can't make copies of the book for all of the students, then make a few sets that the students can take home in turns so that they each have the chance to familiarize themselves with the lives of the people described in the book. Or, as an alternative approach, you could have the students make a poster about a given person and ask them to present their work to the class. If possible, you can then mount the posters on the walls so that the people referred to in this activity actually become a part of the classroom community. In either case, the point is to use a simple grammatical structure and activity to introduce your students to the lives of well-known people so that they share a common body of knowledge that can be referred to in other activities and lessons. You can then use such a context as a vehicle for language practice without having your students be distracted by new vocabulary and cultural information.

If your students have access to the Internet, the site www.biography.com will provide them with the biographical information on hundreds of well-known figures.

1.3. Nonprogressive Verbs

> **Second identity; L, S; ii**
> **Materials included**

To complete this activity, the students need to be familiar with categories such as the following, which are commonly used to describe nonprogressive verbs: sense words, states of mind, emotions, possession, and other. You may need to take some time to have your students practice grouping lists of nonprogressive verbs according to the categories used in this activity. Once the students are comfortable categorizing nonprogressive verbs, brainstorm a list of well-known people, living or dead, with whom the students are familiar. (Ideally, you would be able to refer to the people your class discussed when completing activity 1.2.) Then have the students write in the names of these people in the grid found in Appendix 1.3a. Next, have the students write the infinitive form of the nonprogressive verbs they'd like to work with in the appropriate category as shown in the table.

	Sense Words	States of Mind	Emotions	Possession	Other
Bill Gates	to hear	to believe	to want	to belong	to need
van Gogh	to see	to know	to dislike	to own	to matter

If you don't want to have the students take time to categorize the non-progressive verbs, simply give the students the completed grid found in Appendix 1.3b; however, if you do so, you'll want to make sure that they are familiar with the lives of the people listed in the activity. If they are not, you may prefer to make a grid that lists people with whom your students are more familiar. Before the students begin the exercise, point out that *can* is sometimes used with sense words such as *hear, see, feel, smell,* and *taste.* You may also want to take the time to explain that the following verbs are generally used in the nonprogressive form when they have the following meanings: *appear* and *look*—to seem; *have*—to possess something; *see*—to understand; *think* and *feel*—to have an opinion about something.

Have the students refer to one another's grids to form questions about a given person. The student responding to the questions should take on the persona of someone on the list. Also, contextualize the situation by clarifying where the person is. For example, in this case, Bill Gates (referred to in activity 1.2) could be in his Microsoft office ready to give an interview. A student who has taken on the identity of Bill Gates might be asked:

1. What do/can you hear?
2. What do you believe?
3. What do you want?
4. What belongs to you?
5. What do you need?

And the other student would respond in the first-person point of view. In this case, "Gates" might answer:

1. I can hear computers.
2. I believe in the future of computer technology.
3. I want to be a world leader in computers.
4. A large company belongs to me.
5. I need to make new computer programs.

The purpose of this activity is simply to provide a context for the use of the nonprogressive verbs; however, since people generally don't ask a series of questions using nonprogressive verbs, you may want to have your students add questions that use simple present or present progressive verbs.

Again, remind the students that if they are asking or answering questions about a person who is no longer living, they will need to imagine that the person is actually alive to take part in the interview! In the case of van Gogh (referred to in activity 1.2), a student might ask van Gogh, who is standing out in a field painting:

1. What do/can you see?
2. What do you know about art?
3. What do you dislike?
4. What do you own?
5. What matters to you?

And "van Gogh" might answer:

1. I can see crows flying over fields of corn.
2. I know that art is important.
3. I dislike answering questions.
4. I own a few paintings.
5. Painting matters to me.

1.4. Nonprogressive Verbs

> **Visual focus; L, S; ii**
> **Materials included**

If you want a quick way to practice nonprogressive verbs, bring in pictures that are rich in context and then have the students use nonprogressive verbs to describe the experiences of one of the characters in the illustration. Have the students take on the identity of a given character. In pairs, the students can ask one another questions using nonprogressive verbs such as, "What can/do you see?" and "What can/do you hear?" etc. Referring to the illustration found in Appendix 1.4, a student could imagine himself or herself as a person who is blowing out the candles on the birthday cake and answer, "I can see a beautiful cake with candles on it. I can hear my friends singing 'Happy Birthday to You!' I can smell the candle wax and the cake." Before the students ask one another their questions, give them the chance to simply describe what they actually see in the picture so that they are familiar with the vocabulary terms necessary to talk about the illustration.

1.5. Progessive and Nonprogressive Verbs

> **Visual focus; L, S, W; ii & iiiii**
> **Materials included**

Bring in a set of pictures and/or advertisements that depict individual characters or groups of people. Look for pictures with odd situations. First ask the students to describe the actions of people in the pictures using the simple present and the present progressive. You can have students come up with sentences in pairs and then discuss the results as a class.

Once your students are comfortable describing a given picture, then ask them to tell what the people in the picture are thinking to themselves. At this point, you may want to remind the students that the verb *to think* is a nonprogressive verb when it means *to have an opinion about something* but that the verb can be progressive when it is used to describe someone's thoughts. So, for the purposes of this exercise, students can choose to use the progressive or nonprogressive form of *to think* depending on their intent. Be sure to tell students that their responses should make sense based on the context provided in the picture. For instance, for the illustration of a birthday party found in Appendix 1.4, students might say of a young girl blowing out the candles, "She's thinking (or she thinks) that it's a wonderful birthday party" or "She's thinking (or she thinks) that the candles look beautiful." You may also want to point out that people often leave out the clause word *that* when they are speaking informally. This happens after verbs such as *think, know, hope, believe,* and after adjectives as in phrases such as *I'm happy, I'm glad, It's funny,* and *I'm surprised.* Once the students have worked with the verb *to think,* you can then have them try using these verbs and adjectives to describe a person's thoughts and feelings—for example, "She knows she will open her presents soon. She's glad that it's her birthday."

For a variation of this activity, bring in cartoons with the words in the speech balloons whited out or with empty speech balloons drawn in as necessary (refer to Appendix 1.5 for a sample cartoon). Again, first ask the students to describe the events taking place in the cartoon using the present tense. Then ask them to imagine the private thoughts of each person or character in the cartoon. Have them write these thoughts in the speech balloons or by the corresponding numbers. In pairs or as a class, they can then reveal the private thoughts of the cartoon characters. For this activity, students do not necessarily have to understand the caption or wording that may accompany the original cartoon. They can just make up a scenario based on the situations depicted.

1.6. Progressive Verbs and Using *Probably*

Time zones; L, S; ii & iiiii
Materials included

Draw a set of seven circles on the board. Make the first circle a clock showing the time rounded off to the nearest hour for wherever you are located. For example, if you are teaching in the United States and it is 11:45 in the morning, make a clock face that reads 12:00 noon. With the students' help, fill in the times for various points as you go clockwise around the world. You may want to focus on parts of the world where your students are from or simply use the ready-made set of clocks found in Appendix 1.6. The Appendix also provides a breakdown of international time zones.

Then have the students practice asking one another in pairs, "It's 12:30 in the afternoon here. What time is it in _____?" substituting the names of the countries and the times written on the board. After the students have become comfortable with this information, ask them what they are doing at the present moment. Elicit an answer using the progressive tense such as "We're learning English." Then have the students ask one another questions about what people in the various countries are doing at the present moment. Encourage the students to come up with a number of likely activities for each country—everyday activities as well as events related to local events and politics. Once the students understand the time relationships between countries, you can have them change the time: "It's now 6:00 in the evening here. What time is it in _____? What are people in _____ doing now?" This activity provides a good opportunity for students from different countries to share what is going on in their hometowns at a given time. You can also have students practice using the word *probably* in their responses.

1.7. The Simple Present and Present Progressive

Autobiography; L, S, W; i & iiiii

Ask the students to imagine that they are writing a short account of their lives using the first-person point of view but instruct them to write through the eyes of themselves at periods of five years throughout their lifetimes. They will start writing as if they were a newborn and describe their experiences at that age using the present tense: *It feels good to be held; My father rocks me in a chair; I am angry because I can't speak, so I cry.* Then they can write at the ages of 7, 14, 21, 28, and so on, writing three to five sentences for each age. (If your students are younger, you may want to shorten the span of years.) Ask the students to write using verbs, nouns, and adjectives that help to individualize themselves. Also, remind them that since they are writing as if they really were at a certain age, they should use the simple present and/or present progressive tenses. (This activity can be linked to activity 6.1.)

Since some students do not like revealing personal information, you can choose to apply this activity to the life of a famous person. If you have already done activities 1.2 and 1.3 with the students, then simply refer to the list of people you have already generated with your students. If not, then brainstorm a list of famous people who have lived more than forty years. In either case, ask the students to take on the persona of a famous person and write as if they were that person at various stages of his or her life. You may want to give the students homework time to research information about the person they've chosen to write about. When the students share the "autobiographies" orally with the class, ask the other students to guess whose life is being described.

If your students have read fictional works in English, you can have them use their imaginations to write about a character's experiences at different points in his or her life or at different points in a given story.

Extended Lessons

1.8. The Simple Present and Time Clauses: Poem

1.8a. Presentation

> Sentence completion; L, S, W; ii & iiiii
> Materials included
> 15 minutes/Homework

This lesson is based on a poem by William Shakespeare (1564–1616). Although much of the language used in the poem is more common to the late sixteenth century than to modern usage, the poem can nevertheless be used to illustrate the use of time clauses in English. If you think that your students will be confused by the style of English used in this poem, then I would advise choosing another activity. However, you may find that your students find the contrast interesting. Also, it is helpful for students to be aware that the English language has changed throughout the centuries and that it is in fact changing now. Additionally, many students take pleasure in knowing that they've read an unsimplified work by Shakespeare.

To introduce William Shakespeare's poem "When Icicles Hang by the Wall," write the title of the poem on the board and ask the students to think of ways to finish the sentence using images associated with winter. For example:

When icicles hang by the wall . . .

the lake freezes.
I wear warm clothes.
we make a fire in our fireplace.
my friends and I go ice-skating.

Tell the students that they will be reading a poem that Shakespeare wrote in 1598. As a class, discuss what life was probably like during an English winter at that time. Then give the students a copy of the work sheet in Appendix 1.8a and explain that the following activities are described in Shakespeare's poem. Point out that some of the expressions were commonly used at the time Shakespeare wrote the poem but are not commonly used today. In pairs or as a class, the students should try to come up with a definition for each of the following expressions. (To save class time, have the students prepare their definitions at home.) Students needn't write a definition: they could also come up with a synonymous expression, and/or they could also mime or draw something that represents a definition of a given expression. The words set in boldface type have been glossed to aid the students in the understanding of the text.

When icicles hang by the wall . . .

1. I blow on my nails.
2. I bear logs into **the hall.**
3. my blood is nipped by the cold.
4. we roast **crab apples** in the fire.
5. milk comes home frozen in the pail.
6. she **keels** the pot.
7. birds brood in the snow.
8. the wind **doth** blow.

9. **Ways be foul.**
10. my nose looks red and raw.
11. **the staring owl** sings.

Here are examples of possible definitions the students might come up with.

When icicles hang by the wall . . .

1. I blow hot air on my fingers to warm them.
2. I carry wood into the house.
3. my blood feels cold.
4. we cook crab apples in the fire.
5. the milk in the pail gets so cold it freezes before I get inside.
6. she stirs something cooking in the pot to cool it.
7. birds sit sadly and/or quietly in the snow.
8. the wind blows.
9. the roads/paths are bad.
10. my nose looks red and sore.
11. an owl with large eyes sings.

1.8b. Practice

> **Sequencing; R; ii & iiiii**
> **Materials included**
> **20+ minutes**

Ask the students to read the poem together in pairs (see Appendix 1.8b for a copy of the poem). Discuss any additional vocabulary questions as a class. Then, as a class, ask the students to identify all the actions that occur in the *when* clauses found in each stanza. To check the students' comprehension of the sequenced actions, ask the following questions. Write the answers on the board using either the language used in the poem or more modern English.

STANZA I
- What happens when icicles hang by the wall?

Dick blows on his nails.
Tom bears logs into the hall.
Milk comes home frozen in the pail.
Blood is nipped. (by the cold)
Roads are bad.

- Then what happens?

    The staring owl sings.

- What action occurs at the same time as all actions and situations described in the stanza? (i.e., What is happening at the same time that Dick blows on his nails; Tom bears logs into the fire; milk comes home frozen in the pail; blood is nipped; and roads are bad?)

    Joan keels/stirs the pot.

STANZA II

- What happens when the wind blows?

    People cough.
    Birds sit quietly in the snow.
    Marian's nose looks red.
    Crab apples hiss in the bowl.

- Then what happens?

    The staring owl sings.

- What action occurs at the same time as all actions and situations described in the stanza?

    Joan keels/stirs the pot.

1.8c. Application

> **Time clauses; W; i & iii+**
> **Materials included**
> **15–20 minutes/Homework**

After the students feel comfortable with the time sequence used in the poem, explain that they will write a seasonal poem using an extended *when* clause followed by clauses beginning with *then* and *while* just as Shakespeare did. For this part of the lesson, number the students off 1, 2, 3, and 4. Ask the students to remember who is in their original group of four. Then, have all the number one's get into a large group to write about summer, the number two's group to write about fall, and so on. To make their writing follow the poem's order, have them use the outline in Appendix 1.8c. (You may need to take class time to discuss seasonal changes before students complete the activity.) To save classroom time, you may want to have the students complete their portion of the work sheet as homework. Please note that the students should feel free to reword the prompts found on the work sheet and that each set forms one sentence as in the poem.

When the groups have completed their task, have the students return to their original groups of four to share what they have written for their respective season. Finally, have the students write a seasonal poem following the time sequence outlined on the work sheet and in Shakespeare's poem (though they needn't worry about rhyming words or having two stanzas). Encourage the students to make artwork to accompany their poems.

1.9. The Simple Present and Present Progressive: Haiku

1.9a. Presentation and Practice

> Questions and answers; L, S, R; ii & iiiii
> 20 minutes

You can use haiku poems as a means of helping students to understand the use of verb tenses. Haiku poetry comes from Japanese literature and is generally written in three unrhymed lines consisting of seven syllables: the first line is five syllables, the second seven syllables, and the third five again. However, when these poems are written in English, this pattern is not strictly followed. Generally, haiku poems focus on concrete images from nature and on an aspect of time. Haikus are simple yet profound.

Look for haikus that use the tense you are studying with your students, in this case, the present and present progressive. Write the haiku poem on the board. Preteach any new vocabulary. Then ask the students questions that clarify the sequence of the action. Depending on the level of your students, you can ask more complex questions that require the use of the past and future tenses, for example:

> Wind-blown leaves pirouette
> twirling downwards
> autumn's ballet.
> —Mary Ziemer

- What is the wind doing?
- What is happening to the leaves?
- What time of year is it?
- What is going to happen in the near future?
- How are our lives like the leaves?

Once you have modeled the activity, have the students work in pairs to ask and answer questions about the following haiku. Discuss the results as a class. (Sample questions are listed after the haiku.)

> Desert stones
> reflecting light
> from the moon.
> —Mary Ziemer

- Where are the stones?
- Is it daytime or nighttime? How do you know?
- What do you know about the moon?
- What verb has the writer left out for poetic effect? (to be: are reflecting)

I have used my own haiku as a model, but you may prefer to find translations of haiku poems by Japanese writers such as Kaga no Chiyo (1703–75), Kobayashi Issa (1763–1827), and Matsuo Bashō (1644–94), who is known to have said that "Haiku is simply what is happening in this place at this moment."

1.9b. Application

> **Writing haiku; W; i & ii & iii+ & iiiii**
> **25 minutes/Homework**

You can write your own haiku as a way of inspiring your students to write their own poems using the tense you would like them to practice. Have the students write their haikus and questions on a large piece of paper. Encourage the students to make artwork to accompany their haikus. Then the students can share their haikus and questions in pairs, small groups, and/or as a class.

1.10. The Simple Present: Poem

1.10a. Presentation

> Word association; L, S; i & ii & iiiii
> Materials included
> 15 minutes

In this lesson, students have the opportunity to read a poem by the English poet Alfred, Lord Tennyson (1809–92) and to experience grammatical structures used in a metaphorical way. To prepare students for the content of the poem, write the word *eagle* on the board vertically and, as shown below, write in the expression *the king of birds* using the letter *g* in *eagle* as the *g* in *king*.

E

A

KinG of birds

L

E

Discuss the expression *king of birds* with the students and ask them why they think it might be used to describe the eagle (refer to Appendix 1.10a for a picture of an eagle). The students should comment on the eagle's strength and power. You can explain that the eagle, a bird of prey, has long been admired for its skills in flight and in hunting. Also, just as kings often built their castles on the top of hills, so eagles make their nests in places that are hard to reach, usually in mountainous areas. In ancient times, the Romans associated the eagle with their main god, Jupiter (or Zeus as he's called by the Greeks), whose symbol was a lightning bolt. In more recent history, the bald eagle has served as the national emblem for the United States. (The adjective *bald* refers to the bald eagle's white head as in *piebald,* meaning *marked with white,* and not to a lack of hair or, in this case, feathers!) The eagle is also famous for its large size—female eagles are larger than the males, with a wing span of seven feet (two meters). You may also want to explain that eagles are an endangered species. During the 1970s in the United States, the chemicals sprayed on crops to protect them from insects got into the eagles' food and water supplies, causing their eggshells to be weakened so that many of the eggshells broke before the eagles were ready to hatch. As a result, the eagle population was greatly reduced. Also, their hunting grounds have been reduced as a result of population growth and logging.

Once you've discussed the eagle's characteristics with your students, ask them to copy the word *eagle* onto a piece of paper, writing it vertically as you have on the board. Then ask them to think of nouns, verbs, adjectives, and/or adverbs that share a letter with one of the letters in the word *eagle*. For example, a student might come up with the following word associations.

Endangered species
gr**A**ceful
fli**G**ht
Lightning bolt
hunt**E**r

Give the students a few minutes to work individually. Then you can ask the students to share their results in pairs and finally as a class. During the class discussion, you may want to preteach words found in the poem that your students may not know such as *crag, azure,* and *thunderbolt.* These words are also glossed.

1.10b. Practice

Discourse analysis; L, S, R; i & ii & iiii
Materials included
20–30 minutes/Homework

Since this poem is in the public domain, it may be copied; however, you could also simply dictate the poem to your students. Then have the students read the poem circling and defining all the present tense verbs that are associated with the eagle's actions (see Appendix 1.10b for a copy of the poem). The students should come up with the following.

He clasps the crag.
He stands.
He watches.
He falls.

Some of the students may mistake *crooked, ringed,* and *wrinkled* for past tense verbs. If so, you can point out that these are past participles, forms that are being used as adjectives.

Then ask pairs of students to read the first stanza to answer the questions in Appendix 1.10b for stanza one.

After the students have discussed their responses elicit the following answers from the students.

1. Why does the speaker say the eagle has hands?
   The eagle's claws, or talons, hold onto the crag like the fingers of a hand. (You may want to let the students know that when a poet uses human characteristics to describe something that is not human, then she or he has used the technique of *personification*.)

2. If the sun is over 93 million miles away, how can the eagle be close to the sun?
   Because the eagle's nest is placed high on a crag, it looks close to the sun when a person looks up at it.

3. What color is the eagle surrounded by?
   The eagle is surrounded by the color blue.

Then ask the students to read the second stanza to answer the questions for stanza two.

Elicit the following answers from the students.

4. Why does the sea look wrinkled and as if it's crawling?
   The sea looks this way because it is seen from the eagle's point of view on the mountain. (At this point in the lesson, you may want to share the expression *a bird's eye view* with the students.)

5. What does the eagle's fall remind the speaker of? Why?
   The eagle's fall reminds the speaker of a thunderbolt because it is so powerful and fast. (You may want to remind students of the association with the god Zeus—or Jupiter—and his lightning bolt.)

6. Why does the eagle leave its place on the crag?
   The eagle leaves its place to catch its prey.

7. What might be another word for *fall* in the way that it is used in this poem?
   Another word for *fall* in the poem could be *dive*.

1.10c. Application

> Creature poem; W; i
> 20 minutes/Homework

Ask the students to think of four to six verbs in the present tense that describe characteristic actions of an animal, a bird, a fish, a reptile, or a mythical beast that they would like to write a short poem about. In their poem, they should sequence these verbs in a logical way and describe the creature's natural habitat. Encourage the students to use personification. Stress that they needn't worry about having rhyming words. If you have students who feel intimidated about writing a poem, have them simply write a descriptive paragraph about their topic. In either case, to help the students organize their thoughts, you can have them make a word association list for the creature they've chosen to write about just as they did for the word *eagle*.

1.11. The Present Tense: Definition

1.11a. Presentation

> Definition; L, S, W; i & ii & iiiii
> 10 minutes

This lesson provides students with the opportunity to think about the definition of love while practicing the use of the present tense. Ask the students to make two columns on a blank piece of paper. On the left side, have them write the prompt *Love is. . .* , and on the right hand side, have them write *Love is not. . . .* Then they should use words or phrases to write four possible endings for each of the prompts. After the students have had a few minutes to think of ideas, give pairs of students the opportunity to share what they've written. As a class, discuss the results. Write up the students' responses on the board and guide the discussion in order to elicit the following vocabulary terms that will be found in the practice stage of the activity.

Love is . . .	*Love is not . . .*
patient	impatient
kind	unkind
protective	easily angered
trustful	distrustful
true	untrue or false
persevering	selfish or self-seeking
never failing	happy when bad things happen/revengeful
giving	envious
modest	boastful

Once you've discussed the new vocabulary terms, ask the students to think about some general categories of love. Students might come up with examples such as romantic and erotic love, love between two friends, the love parents have for their children, and the love of God or a Higher Power. Point out to your students that in English it is hard to distinguish between the different ways the word *love* can be used unless it is preceded by an adjective, whereas other languages use different words to express the different kinds of love. For example, in Greek, the word *eros* is used to describe erotic or romantic love, while the term *agape* is used to describe a love that is superhuman and godlike in its goodness. You may find that some of your students have been surprised to hear people in the United States use the word *love* to describe their feelings for chocolate ice cream or a peanut butter sandwich! If you'd like, discuss some of the words for *love* found in the languages your students speak.

1.11b. Practice

Explain to the students that they are going to read a definition of *agape* love from a letter written by Paul of Tarsus (circa A.D. 3–62) to people who lived in a city called Corinth; for this reason, the letter is called Corinthians. This excerpt is taken from New Testament biblical literature.

You can select either Option One or Option Two for the practice stage of this lesson: Option One deals with present tense verbs while Option Two focuses on the use of parallelism as a stylistic device. (*Note:* These materials may be photocopied only if the copyright information is included on the copies.)

Option One

> Cloze; L, S, R; i & ii & iiiii
> Materials included
> 15–20 minutes

As you read the text aloud, simply have the students complete the cloze passage found in Appendix 1.11b, Option One (p. 46). Before you read the passage, give the students the opportunity to read through it circling any words that are new to them. Discuss these vocabulary items as a class. Some of the more difficult words are glossed on the handout.

See if the students can predict which present tense verbs and/or auxiliary verbs should go in the blanks. Once the students are familiar with the excerpt, read the completed passage aloud to the students and have them try to fill in the blanks. After the first reading, let the students compare their results in pairs. Read the passage again and then check the students' responses as a class.

The key to the cloze is as follows.

1. am
2. have
3. give
4. gain
5. does

6. is
7. rejoices
8. hopes
9. fails

If you prefer, instead of reading the cloze passage aloud, simply write up the missing verbs on the board and ask the students to match up the appropriate verb with its corresponding blank.

Option Two

> **Parallelism; R, W; i & ii & iiii**
> **Materials included**
> **15–25 minutes**

This option gives students the opportunity to become familiar with the stylistic technique of parallelism that is often used in English.

Explain that the passage uses a stylistic device known as *parallelism*. Take a moment to help your students understand the term *parallel* by drawing the following sets of figures on the board and asking the students to identify the parallel lines.

a. ┼   **b.** ═   **c.** ∟   **d.** ∧

The students should identify example b as being parallel. You can also point out that the word *parallel* has three parallel lines in it (the letters *L*). Just as two parallel lines are evenly balanced and mirror one another, so writers use different parts of speech so that they parallel one another, as in the following examples.

Words:	Love is <u>patient</u> and <u>kind.</u>
Phrases:	I am thinking of you. I think of you <u>in the morning, in the afternoon</u> and <u>in the evening.</u>
Dependent clauses:	<u>When you spoke to me the first time</u> and <u>when you laughed,</u> I heard the voice of love.
Sentences:	<u>I need you, I adore you, I love you.</u> (When sentences are parallel, they are sometimes written with commas or semicolons between them rather than a period.)

You can write these sentences on the board and ask the students to underline the parallel elements. Once you feel your students have a general understanding of parallelism, prepare them to read through the cloze passage in Appendix 1.11b, Option Two (p. 47). First, have the students circle all the present tense verbs and discuss their meaning if necessary. Second, ask the students to underline any new vocabulary words and discuss these as a class.

Then explain that to complete this passage, they should first familiarize themselves with the words listed at the top of the passage and in the excerpt. Some of the more difficult words are glossed on the handout. Next, they should read through the cloze exercise and determine where each term belongs by matching up the word with its parallel structure in the passage. Have the students work individually or in pairs to complete the excerpt.

The key to the cloze is as follows.

1. clanging
2. knowledge
3. If
4. nothing
5. is

6. not
7. it
8. protects
9. always

After the students have completed the passage, have them put rectangles around the parallel elements. When they finish, they will see that the author has used parallelism throughout the passage.

1.11c. Application

> Definition; L, S, W; i & iiiii
> Materials included
> 20 minutes/Homework

Whichever option you have chosen for the practice stage, in the application stage, take a few minutes to discuss the students' reactions to this definition of *agape* love. Do they agree or disagree with this definition? Would they like to add something to it or take something away? Can they give an example of kindness or patience? Is it difficult to always be so loving? Why or why not?

Once you've discussed the passage on love, ask the students to write a paragraph in which they give their own definition of love. Encourage them to use the new vocabulary terms they learned in the lesson. In their definitions ask them to give examples of love. The students should try to use numerous present tense verbs in their paragraph. And, if they are familiar with other definitions of love, have them write about these as well. If your students have completed Option Two, suggest that they try to use parallel structures in their writing.

If you'd like, you can have your students write a definition of another abstract concept such as *hate* or *guilt* or, on the more positive side, *justice, freedom, equality, innocence,* or *joy.* Students may also want to focus on concepts from other Wisdom Traditions such as *mindfulness,* which is defined in the Buddhist scriptures; *purposelessness,* which is an important concept in Taoism; *filial piety,* which is foregrounded in Confucianism; *taqwa,* meaning *to guard against danger,* a quality described in the Islamic book of the Koran as the development of *inner morality;* and *shalom,* or *peace,* which is characteristic of Judaism.

If you'd like your students to write more than a paragraph, you could have them write a short essay based on an outline such as the one found in Appendix 1.11c.

Before the students begin their work, you could have them first write out a list of words that describe what their topic is and what it is not as was done for the word *love* in the presentation stage.

If you have time and access to the sound track of the movie *Blue* directed by Krzysztof Kieslowski, you may want to have your students listen to the "Song for the Unification of Europe (Julie's Version)" by Zbigniew Preisner (©1993 MK2/Virgin France S.I.A.E.). The chorus sings the excerpted passage on love in Greek. You can have your students listen to the music and have them think of it as a tone poem. Then they can write or discuss whether or not they think the music conveys the tone of the passage on love. The translated English version of the song lyrics differs slightly from the text used in this lesson, so you could also have your students discuss these differences.

It also is interesting to have your students consider why the composer has chosen to use Greek in a song about the unification of Europe. You can explain that ideas from ancient Greek civilization (from 1100 B.C.) have influenced the development of philosophy, art, architecture, and the sciences in European culture.

If you complete extended lessons 2.11, 3.10c, Option Three (the second excerpted passage), and/or 3.11c with your students, you can then have them compare and contrast the definition of love discussed in 1.11 with the ideas presented in these lessons.

Appendix 1.1. *Yes/No* Questions

1. You want to rent a new apartment. You call the apartment manager to ask him or her for information about the apartment.

2. You are curious about an English teacher you will have next quarter. Your classmate had this teacher before. Ask him or her about the teacher.

3. You are going out on a blind date, and you want more information about your date. Your classmate knows this person. Ask him or her about your blind date.

4. You are traveling to a city in the United States for the first time. Your classmate was in this city before. Ask him or her about the city. Choose a city your classmate knows something about.

5. You are traveling to a country for the first time. Your classmate was in this country before. Ask him or her for some information about the country. Choose a country your classmate knows something about.

6. You want to know about a movie. Your classmate recently saw it. Ask him or her about the film. Choose a movie your classmate knows something about.

7. You are interested in buying a new car, but first you want to ask the salesperson some questions about it.

Appendix 1.3a. Stative Verbs

Name(s)_____

	Sense Words	States of Mind	Emotions	Possession	Other
Bill Gates	to hear	to believe	to want	to belong	to need

Appendix 1.3b. Stative Verbs

	Sense Words	*States of Mind*	*Emotions*	*Possession*	*Other*
Bill Gates	to hear	to believe	to want	to belong	to need
The President of the United States	to taste	to suppose	to love	to own	to matter
Madonna	to hear	to remember	to like	to belong	to exist
John Lennon	to feel	to know	to hate	to have	to appear
Elizabeth Taylor	to smell	to prefer	to love	to have	to matter
Frédéric Chopin	to hear	to understand	to like	to own	to need
Michael Jackson	to hear	to realize	to love	to have	to exist

Appendix 1.4. Illustration

Appendix 1.5. Cartoon

Name(s)_____

1.

2.

3.

Appendix 1.6. International Time Zones

| 12:00 noon Los Angeles, U.S.A. | 3:00 P.M. New York, U.S.A. | 9:00 P.M. Zurich, Switzerland | 1:00 A.M. Bombay, India | 4:00 A.M. Peking, China | 5:00 A.M. Tokyo, Japan | 7:00 A.M. Honolulu, Hawaii |

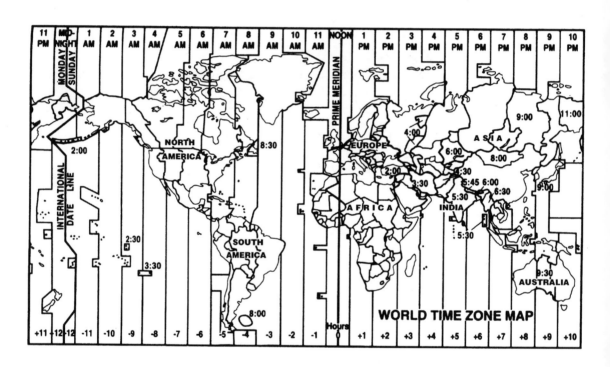

Appendix 1.8a. Shakespeare: Vocabulary

Name(s) _____

Sentences similar to the following are found in a poem by William Shakespeare entitled "When Icicles Hang by the Wall." Try to determine their meanings using the context and/or a dictionary to help you. Each sentence begins with *When icicles hang by the wall. . . .*

Shakespeare wrote using poetic language and expressions that were commonly used in the 1500s. Rewrite the sentences in your own words using modern English or else try to mime or to draw the meaning of an expression. The first one has been done for you.

When icicles hang by the wall . . .

1. I blow on my nails.

   I blow hot air on my fingers to warm them. _____

2. I bear logs into **the hall.**

   _____

3. my blood is nipped by the cold.

   _____

4. we roast **crab apples** in the fire.

   _____

5. milk comes home frozen in the pail.

   _____

6. she **keels** the pot.

   _____

7. birds brood in the snow.

   _____

8. the wind **doth** blow.

   _____

----

the hall: A large room was also called a hall.
crab apples: A type of apple that is cooked over a fire. When the apples get hot, they make a hissing sound.
to keel: to stir something
doth: does

9. **ways be foul.**

_____

10. my nose looks red and raw.

_____

11. **The staring owl** sings.

_____

_____

ways be foul: Roads and paths are in a bad condition.
the staring owl: _The_ is used to refer to a specific owl that the speaker of the poem is thinking of or to a general
type of owl that is seen in winter with its eyes wide open.

Appendix 1.8b. Poem

William Shakespeare (1564–1616)

WHEN ICICLES HANG BY THE WALL (1598)

When icicles hang by the wall,
   And Dick the shepherd blows his nail,
And Tom bears logs into the hall,
   And milk comes frozen home in pail,
When blood is nipped and ways be foul,
   Then nightly sings the staring owl:
     "Tu-whit, to-who!"
    A merry note,
While greasy Joan doth keel the pot.

When all aloud the wind doth blow,
   And coughing drowns **the parson's saw,**
And birds sit brooding in the snow,
   And Marian's nose looks red and raw,
When roasted **crabs** hiss in the bowl,
   Then nightly sings the staring owl:
     "Tu-whit, to-who!"
    A merry note,
While greasy Joan doth keel the pot.

---

the parson's saw: A *parson* is another word for a preacher or a teacher in a Protestant church. A *saw* is used to cut wood. So, the things that the preacher is saying sound like an old saw going back and forth.
crabs: crab apples—a kind of apple that can be cooked over a fire

Appendix 1.8c. Seasons   Name(s)_____

1. **Summer**

   When the sun shines hot in the sky,

   And

   Then

   While

2. **Fall**

   When the leaves fall from the trees,

   And

   Then

   While

3. **Winter**

When frost makes curtains on the windows,

And

Then

While

4. **Spring**

When flowers bloom in the fields,

When

Then

While

Appendix 1.10a. An Eagle

Appendix 1.10b. Poem   Name(s)_____

Alfred, Lord Tennyson (1809–1892)

THE EAGLE

He clasps the **crag** with crooked hands;
Close to the sun in lonely lands,
Ringed with the **azure** world, he stands.

The wrinkled sea beneath him crawls;
He watches from his mountain walls,
And like **a thunderbolt** he falls.

Questions for stanza one:

1. Why does the speaker say that the eagle has *hands?*

2. If the sun is over ninety-three million miles away, how can the eagle be *close to the sun?*

3. What color is the eagle surrounded by?

Questions for stanza two:

4. Why does the sea look wrinkled and as if it's crawling?

5. What does the eagle's fall remind the speaker of? Why?

6. Why does the eagle leave its place on the crag?

7. What might be another word for *fall* in the way that it is used in this poem?

The poem "The Eagle" is in the public domain. Questions © 1999 University of Michigan

---

crag: a sharp edge of a cliff or mountain peak
azure: blue
a thunderbolt: a flash of lightning along with the sound of thunder

Appendix 1.11b, Option One. Cloze: The Present Tense

Name(s)_____

I Corinthians 13:1–7

If I speak with the tongues of men and of angels, but have not

love, I (1) _____ only **a resounding gong** or **a clanging**

cymbal. If I (2) _____ **the gift of prophecy** and can

understand all mysteries, and all knowledge, and if I have a faith

that can **move mountains,** but have not love, I am nothing. If I

(3) _____ all I have to the poor and **offer my life as a**

sacrifice for others, but have not love, I (4) _____

nothing. Love is patient, love is kind. It (5) _____ not

envy, it does not boast, it is not proud. It is not rude, it is not

self-seeking, it (6) _____ not easily angered, it

keeps no record of wrongs. Love does not delight in evil but

(7) _____ with the truth. It always protects, always

trusts, always (8) _____, always perseveres. Love never

(9) _____.

This exercise is based on material adapted from the *New Revised Standard Version Bible.* Exercise © 1999
University of Michigan

---

a resounding gong: a round metal disk that makes a loud sound when it is hit with a padded hammer
a clanging cymbal: a brass instrument that makes sharp tones when struck with a drumstick
the gift of prophecy: the ability to tell what will happen in the future
to move mountains: to do something that seems impossible to do
to offer one's life as a sacrifice for others: to suffer and/or die so that someone else does not have to suffer
and/or die

Appendix 1.11b, Option Two. Cloze: Parallelism

Name(s) _____

I Corinthians 13:1–7

protects	is	clanging
not	it	knowledge
nothing	If	always

If I speak with the tongues of men and of angels, but have not

love, I am only **a resounding gong** or a (1) _____

cymbal. If I have the **gift of prophecy** and can understand all

mysteries, and all (2) _____, and if I have **a faith**

that can move mountains, but have not love, I am nothing.

(3) _____ I give all I have to the poor and **offer**

my life as a sacrifice for others, but have not love, I gain

(4) _____. Love is patient, love (5) _____

kind. It does not envy, it does not boast, it is (6) _____

proud. It is not rude, it is not self-seeking, (7) _____

is not easily angered, it keeps no record of wrongs. Love

does not delight in evil but rejoices with the truth. It always

(8) _____, always trusts, always hopes,

(9) _____ perseveres. Love never fails.

This exercise is based on material adapted from the *New Revised Standard Version Bible*. Exercise © 1999
University of Michigan

a resounding gong: a round metal disk that makes a loud sound when it is hit with a padded hammer
a cymbal: a brass instrument that makes sharp tones when struck with a drumstick
the gift of prophecy: the ability to tell what will happen in the future
a faith that can move mountains: a belief that one can do what seems impossible
to offer one's life as a sacrifice for others: to suffer and/or die so that someone else does not have to suffer
and/or die

Appendix 1.11c. Definition Paper: An Abstract Term

Name(s) _____

Use this outline to write an essay about an abstract term. Imagine that the people who will read your essay know nothing about the meaning of the word that you have chosen to write about.

Paragraph 1: In your own words, define the term you are going to write about and explain why it is important for people to understand this term.

Paragraph 2: Give examples from everyday life that show the meaning of the term you have defined. You may also want to give examples from history.

Paragraph 3: Define a term that means the opposite of the word you have chosen to write about. *Or,* define a word or words that are similar in meaning to the word you have defined in your paper but that are not exactly the same.

Paragraph 4: Predict how the term you have defined will influence or change the world in the future.

Chapter 2
The Past Tense

Itemized Reference List

Skill Areas		Group Work	
Listening	L	Individual	i
Speaking	S	Pair	ii
Reading	R	Small Group	iii+
Writing	W	Class	iiiii

Structure		Activity	Skills	Groups	Appendix
Supplementary Activities					
2.1.	The Simple Past and Past Progressive	Fables	L, S, R, W	i & iii+	69
2.2.	The Simple Past	Time lines	L, S, R, W	i & ii	70
2.3.	The Simple Past and Past Progressive	Chain story	L, S, R, W	iii+ & iiiii	
2.4.	The Past Progressive	Record keeping	L, S, W	i & ii & iii+ & iiiii	71
2.5.	The Simple Past and Past Progressive	Retrospective	L, S, R, W	i & iii+ & iiiii	
2.6.	*Used to* and the Past Tense	Fads and trends	L, S, W	i & iii+ & iiiii	72
2.7.	*Used to* and the Past Tense	Picture story	L, S, W	i & ii & iiiii	73
Extended Lessons					
2.8.	The Past Tense and Using Time Clauses: Scenarios				
2.8a.	Presentation	Realia	L, S	iiiii	
2.8b.	Practice	Visualization	L, S	ii & iiiii	
2.8c.	Application	Story	W	i	
2.9.	The Simple Past and Question Words: Travel Itinerary				
2.9a.	Presentation	Itinerary	L, S	iiiii	75
2.9b.	Practice	Itinerary	L, S, R, W	i & ii	
2.9c.	Application	Travel log	L, S, R, W	i & iii+ & iiiii	
2.10.	The Simple Past and Past Progressive: History				
2.10a.	Presentation	Historical time line	L, S, R	iii+	77
2.10b.	Practice	Historical clock	L, S, R	ii	
2.10c.	Application	Research	W	i & iii+ & iiiii	
2.11.	The Simple Past: Poem				
2.11a.	Presentation	Word families	L, S, R, W	i & ii & iiiii	
2.11b.	Practice	Sequencing	R, W	i & iii+	80
2.11c.	Application	Prose writing	L, S, W	i & iiiii	

Supplementary Activities

2.1. The Simple Past and Past Progressive

Fables; L, S, R, W; i & iii+
Materials included

Use fables as a way to practice the past tense. You may want to inform your students that a fable is a brief story that teaches the listener or reader a lesson. This lesson is called a moral, and a moral is generally stated in one sentence. Fables come from around the world and have a rich history. For example, in ancient Greece, fables were used as a way to criticize political leaders. In Rome, the emperor Marcus Aurelius (A.D. 161–80) collected over 300 fables. In Asia and India, the Buddha (A.D. 563?–483?) is said to have used fables to teach moral lessons. Look for fables that use the past form. Make a strip story of the fable and give each student, in groups of seven or more, one portion of the story. (See Appendix 2.1 for sample strip stories. The fable "The Wind and the Sun" is believed to be of Greek origin while "The Dog and the Reflection" is thought to be of Indian origin.) Before the groups try to put a fable in order, give the students time to make sure they understand the vocabulary in their portion of the story. You can give each group the same fable or different ones and see which group finishes first. Once the students have completed a fable, have them make a moral for it (using the present tense to express a general truth). You can also have the students apply the moral to real life. Have the students try to reconstruct the fable in writing without referring to the strip story. After this activity, it's interesting to have the students write short fables from their own countries using the past tense. You can then ask the students to make strip stories to use in class.

2.2. The Simple Past

Time lines; L, S, R, W; i & ii
Materials included

Use time lines that outline the lives of cultural figures as a speaking and/or writing prompt to elicit the simple past. Before the students discuss a time line, have them think about anything they might already know about the person to be discussed. Then have the students write questions that address the information found in the time line. In pairs, they can ask one another questions about a person's life using the past tense. A time line with just a few dates can generate a good deal of discussion. Additionally, time lines provide a skeletal framework for the introduction of new vocabulary associated with a given person's life, making it easier to develop lessons that integrate biographical information. For example, consider a short time line that follows the life of Emily Dickinson, an American poet.

When discussing the life of Emily Dickinson with your students, you may want to point out that Emily lived in her family home in Amherst for her entire life, except for one year when she went away to college. Although Dickinson is often thought of as having been a recluse, she kept up a correspondence with her friends and also won a local bread-baking contest. In 1862, Emily wrote to a friend and said that she had recently written her first four verses.

Writes over one thousand poems; only seven are published during her lifetime.

1830	1862	1886	1890
Born in Amherst, Massachusetts	Writes her first four poems	Dies	A volume of her poetry is published.

Sample Questions

1. When was Emily Dickinson born?
2. Where was she born?
3. When did she write her first poem?
4. How many poems did she write during her lifetime?
5. How many poems did she publish during her lifetime?
6. When did she die?
7. When was the first book of her poems published?
8. Do you think she was famous during her lifetime?

After you've introduced the life of Emily Dickinson to your students, you can readily refer to her poetry in an extended lesson.

You will find additional time lines in Appendix 2.2. These time lines are based on the lives of well-known people from the United States. (The time line that refers to Martin Luther King, Jr., is further developed in activity 7.2 and extended lessons 3.11 and 7.6.) Once the students have completed this activity, ask each of them to make a time line about a famous person from their respective countries. Make sure that students write the information in the time line using the present tense so that their classmates will get practice changing the verbs into the past when forming questions about the time line. You may want to give the students time outside of class to research information for their time lines.

2.3. The Simple Past and Past Progressive

> **Chain story; L, S, R, W; iii+ & iiiii**

Put the students into groups of five or more and give each student a piece of paper on which you have written the line *I'm sorry I was late, but I* . . . . This student must use the simple past or past progressive to write a completion for the excuse and then pass the paper on to the next person. This person can read the excuse (silently) and either continue it or make up another one. After this, she or he should fold the paper just enough so that the next student can read only the line just written. Then, on the same piece of paper, the third student can either continue the excuse or make up a new one, passing it on to the next student, again folding the paper so that only the previous line can be read. Each person in the group should start a chain so that the students are continually writing lines for stories until everyone has written at least one line of each story. Encourage the students to think of unusual excuses. When the groups have completed their stories, ask each group member to read the story she or he has ended up with to the others. The groups can then choose the funniest one to share with the class.

Another version of this activity can start with the line *A funny thing happened to me on the way to class* . . . .

2.4. The Past Progressive

> **Record keeping; L, S, W; i & ii & iii+ & iiiii**
> **Materials included**

With your students, brainstorm idiomatic expressions that are related to the concept of time such as the following.

    Time flies.
    Time is money.
    To spend time with someone
    To kill time

To waste time
The time of your life
Time out
Time marches on.

If your students are unfamiliar with such idioms, then write them up on the board and give the students the chance to discuss in pairs what these idioms might mean. Use these idioms for the basis of a brief class discussion about the concept of time as it is understood in English-speaking countries where such idioms are commonly used. You may also want to spend some time discussing other perceptions of time such as *timelessness, eternal time,* when *time stands still,* and when *time drags.* Encourage the students to bring up idioms related to time that are common in their native languages.

Ask your students how many times a day they check to see what the time is. Explain to them that throughout the following day, they should use the chart in Appendix 2.4 to keep track of how many times they checked the time and what they were doing each time they looked at a watch or clock. Ask the students to use either the simple past or past progressive when they fill out the information in the chart. The next day, conduct an informal survey to find out who checked the time the most and least often. In small groups, have the students find the answers to questions such as, What kinds of things were people doing when they checked the time? Are there any similarities? Did people look at a wristwatch or wall clock to check the time? Did they ask other people for the time? Did they check the time when they were in a hurry? Did this activity make them more aware of the passing time? Before the groups begin their discussions, you may want to review how to say different times in English.

After a few minutes, have a representative from each group report back to the class. If you would like to extend this activity to time clauses, you can have students write up a report about their results. Explain that the students do not need to refer to specific times but can use time clauses to express their results as in the following.

- When I woke up, I checked the time. During my English class, I checked the time twice.
- While I was working on the computer, I looked at the clock three times.

You can also have the students write a paragraph about how they experience the concept of time in their own lives.

2.5. The Simple Past and Past Progressive

> **Retrospective; L, S, R, W; i & iii+ & iiiii**

With your students, brainstorm interesting events that took place during the preceding year. You may want to divide your students into groups that focus on fashion, movies, well-known people, political changes, natural disasters, etc. You could also have groups focus on global, national, or local events. To save class time, give students time at home to research their topic. Once the students have gathered information about their topic, put them into new groups made up of one representative from each of the previous groups and ask them to share the information they have gathered. When in groups, the students should elicit the information from one another by asking relevant questions.

If possible, bring in magazines such as *Time* and *People* that do retrospectives every new year and have the students use these articles as sources of information. Using pictures from the magazines, the students can also make a collage about their retrospective and share it with the class. If you don't have access to such publications, you can simply have your students make word clusters around central ideas, for example, consider the deaths of well-known people in 1997.

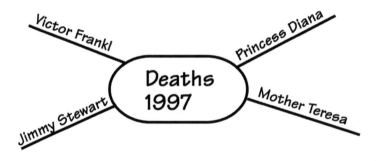

As a follow-up assignment, students can then write a short article about the preceding year. You can have them write not only about the information they gathered for the focus of their retrospective but also about the information gathered by other groups. To do this activity, the students will need to take notes when their classmates are sharing their retrospectives. If it is toward the end of the year when you do this activity with your students, then simply focus on the year that is almost over.

2.6. *Used to* and the Past Tense

> Fads and trends; L, S, W; i & iii+ & iiiii
> Materials included

Have students discuss what fads used to be popular in the 1950s, 1960s, and 1980s. The students can also talk about which fads developed into trends during these decades and are still popular. Point out that not every fad becomes a trend, although fads from different eras may come into fashion now and again. Discuss the idea of being *in* and *out* of fashion; the idea of being *trendy* or being fashionable; and the idea of *changing lifestyles.*

To complete this activity, it is helpful to have small groups of students focus on a particular decade and then report back to the class. Use an overhead projector to display the drawings in Appendix 2.6 as the basis for this activity. During the group work, you can help students with the vocabulary terms that are specific to their decade. It is also helpful to have the students think in terms of categories such as food, fashion, music, movies, games, inventions, popular stars, popular names for children, and popular slang expressions. The students can then share these in groups and/or with the class. Write the words *fad* and *trend* on the board and then write examples of each on the board as the groups report back to the class. Here is an example of how a partial list from the 1950s might look.

Fads	Trends That Developed from These Fads
Fashion	
jeans	jeans
T-shirts	T-shirts
rolled-up pant legs	
poodle skirts	
pony tails	
Food	
fast food	fast food
Music	
rock 'n' roll	rock 'n' roll
Elvis Presley	Elvis Presley

Since the drawings in Appendix 2.6 focus on trends in North American culture, it is also interesting to have the students draw and/or write about fads that were popular in their own countries during different decades and about trends that are still common. In either case, you may want to give the students time outside of class to find out more about their topic.

Once the students have presented their information, you can have them write a short paragraph about the fads and trends related to a specific decade or an essay related to the development of fads and trends in general. Encourage the students to use frequency adverbs as well as *used to* and the past tense in their writing. For an article on this topic, refer to the reading "Trends and Fads" in *Interactions II: A Reading Skills Book,* edited by Elaine Kirn and Pamela Hartmann, pp. 87–89 (New York: McGraw-Hill Companies, 1996). Before you photocopy any of the McGraw-Hill materials be sure to contact them for copyright permission.

2.7. *Used to* and the Past Tense

> **Picture story; L, S, W; i & ii & iiiii**
> **Materials included**

In a set of three boxes, sketch pictures that show (1) What a person used to do, (2) What happened to make him or her change, and (3) How she or he changed as shown in the boxes below. For the drawings in the picture sequence shown below, a student might say, "John used to eat fast food every day, but then he had a heart attack. Now he eats only healthy foods."

| Jim-every day | Heart attack! | Health food |

You will find more picture stories in Appendix 2.7a. The picture stories are all related to experiences common to life in urban settings. You might decide to make picture stories that directly relate to the cultural context in which you are teaching. In either case, you may need to preteach some vocabulary terms associated with the pictures. Once you have modeled the activity, have the students share their stories in pairs and then as a class.

After the students practice the form using the ideas presented in the picture stories in Appendix 2.7a, have them make a few scenarios of their own (see Appendix 2.7b for a blank work sheet). Collect these and use them as the basis for additional prompts.

To extend this into a writing activity, have students write down their sentences and add imaginative details to the story. For example:

> Jim used to eat fast food almost every day. He always ordered french fries and a hamburger. He also used to put a lot of butter on his bread and potatoes. One day, when he was at the beach, he had a heart attack. Luckily, some people were near by and called for help. He had to stay in the hospital for two weeks. Now Jim eats only healthy food. His doctor told him to eat lots of fruits and vegetables. He also exercises more.

Extended Lessons

2.8. The Past Tense and Using Time Clauses: Scenarios

2.8a. Presentation

> Realia; L, S; iiiii
> 10 minutes

To prepare students for the practice of the simple past and the past progressive tenses with time clauses, you can introduce them to a given scenario that they can then use for the basis of their practice. In this case, the scenario is a rock concert. You may need to preteach the term *rock concert.* Discuss how rock concerts are often given in large sports arenas, or stadiums, where a rock band will play for tens of thousands of people. With the students, brainstorm the names of some English-speaking rock bands with which the students may be familiar such as the Beatles, the Rolling Stones, and U2. If any of your students have been to a rock concert, take a few minutes to discuss their impressions of the event. If possible, bring in a poster and tickets for an actual rock concert that has already taken place and use these as the basis for a class discussion. You can also bring in the covers from record albums, tape cassettes or CDs and use these as conversation prompts. If you have a T-shirt from a rock concert, bring this in as well. You can also encourage the students to think about the cultural significance of rock concerts in general and of certain rock concerts in particular. As an example of the latter, consider Woodstock, which came to symbolize the 1960s, Live-Aid, which helped to raise money for the hungry in Africa in the late 1980s, and U2's 1997 concert in Sarajevo, the capital of Bosnia, which signified hope for the people in war-torn Sarajevo.

For this lesson, I have focused on the U2 concert in Sarajevo.

Whichever band and concert you choose to discuss, it is also fun to play one or more of the group's songs for the class before proceeding with the lesson. The idea is to set the scene for the grammar practice activity and to introduce the students to the vocabulary associated with a given scenario.

2.8b. Practice

> Visualization; L, S; ii & iiiii
> 15 minutes

Once the students are comfortable talking about the background information, ask them to imagine what kinds of things people in the audience did while they were waiting for U2 to come out and play. You might come up with a list such as the following.

    talked
    read information about the concert
    smoked a cigarette
    bought food and drinks
    bought a T-shirt

After you've come up with a short list of activities, assign names of your students to a given activity. Also, write up the time clause(s) on the board. For example:

While the audience was waiting for U2 to come out,

    Anita and Sylvia—talked
    Yuki—read information about the concert
    Stephan—smoked a cigarette
    Marek and Peter—bought food and drinks
    Elena—bought a T-shirt

Then, in pairs, have the students use these prompts to ask one another questions about what people in the audience were doing while they were waiting for the band; for example:

    What did Anita and Sylvia do while they were waiting for U2 to come out?
    While the crowd was waiting for U2, what did Anita and Sylvia do?

Next, shift the questions to what happened when U2 came out on stage to play. As a class, discuss how the actions of those in the crowd changed. Write the changes up on the board (but don't erase the information that you've already written up on the board).

When U2 came out on the stage,

> Anita and Sylvia stopped talking.
> Yuki started yelling.
> Stephan lit up another cigarette.
> Marek and Peter stopped eating their hot dogs.
> Elena whistled.
> everyone stood up and clapped.

You can point out that in this case the simple past is used to show that the actions in both clauses lasted for only a short time and happened at the same moment. However, the students could also ask the questions using *while*—"While U2 was coming out on the stage, what did people do?"— but the use of *while* makes it seem like it took a long time for the band to come out on the stage. Have the students ask and answer the questions in pairs.

To refocus the students' attention, ask them what the people in the crowd were doing or did while/when the band was playing. Again, make up a list of actions together and write these up on the board next to the previous sets of prompts.

While U2 was playing,

> Anita and Sylvia sang along.
> Yuki cried.
> Stephan smoked a pack of cigarettes.
> Marek and Peter played air guitar.
> Elena danced.
> everyone listened and had a good time.

In pairs, the students should then ask one another questions about what people were doing while the band was playing.

2.8c. Application

> Story; W; i
> 20+ minutes/Homework

For writing practice, have the students write a story about the rock concert. Essentially, the students should write out the information they discussed in class. At the beginning of their story, they should give background information about the concert. Then they should describe what happened at different times during the concert. When writing their scenarios, the students can refer to the information on the board for help or make up other actions to go with the story. Encourage the students to use their imaginations to describe the band's performance and the crowd's reaction. If they are familiar with the band's music, they can also give their opinion of it.

To round off this stage of the lesson, you could bring in a song by the band your class has focused on in the presentation and practice stages of the lesson and have them analyze the time clauses or the lack thereof. For example, the songs "Trip through Your Wires" and "Matters of the Disappeared" from U2's *Joshua Tree* album (© 1987 Island Records Ltd.) use the past tense. However, neither one of these songs uses time words and clauses, so, if you would like, you could have your students reword the lyrics so that they include a few time clauses.

You could also have the students apply the format of this lesson plan to other situations in life such as a sports match, a wedding, a business meeting/presentation, a surprise birthday party, or an English lesson. Whatever the event, a group of people should be involved in it. The students should set the action in the past and write about what happened at different times during the event they're describing. For example, a student writing about a wedding could write about what people did while they were waiting for the bride to come down the aisle; what happened when she came down the aisle; and what people did while the ceremony was taking place. For an English lesson, a student could write about what people did while they were waiting for the teacher to come into the room; what they did when the teacher came in; and what they did while they were in class. As with the rock concert scenario, have the students give names to the characters involved. Also, have the students give their audience background information about the event they are describing.

2.9. The Simple Past and Question Words: Travel Itinerary

2.9a. Presentation

> Itinerary; L, S; iiiii
> Materials included
> 10 minutes

Tell the students that you are going to present the itinerary of a two-week-long trip you took to London last August. Use Appendix 2.9a, Option One (p. 75), as a source for the trip's itinerary or make your own using the calendar found in Appendix 2.9a, Option Two (p. 76). Establish the present time as being August 15. You returned a few days ago, and the students are going to ask you about your trip. After the students have reviewed your itinerary, have them make questions about your trip using the past tense. You may need to review time expressions used with the past tense such as *two weeks ago, a few days ago.* You may also need to review how to read dates using ordinal numbers. Discuss any new vocabulary with the students. Bring in pictures if possible. Here are some sample questions.

- Where did you go two weeks ago?
- When did you leave for _____?
- What were you doing seven days ago?
- Where were you on the 10th of August?
- Which place did you like best?
- Where did you stay in _____?
- How did you like _____?

Model responses for the students.

2.9b. Practice

> Itinerary; L, S, R, W; i & ii
> Materials included
> 20+ minutes/Homework

Give each student a blank calendar for the first two weeks in the month of August (see Appendix 2.9a, Option Two [p. 76], for a blank calendar) and tell them that they should fill out the calendar with information about an actual or imaginary two-week-long trip that they have taken. Since the students may need to rely on their imaginations rather than on actual experience to write their itineraries, tell them that they can make up names for hotels and restaurants if they need to. It is more interesting, though, if they can refer to travel guides such as the *Let's Go* (© St. Martin's Press) and *The Lonely Planet* (© Lonely Planet Publications) series. Or they can refer to travel guides in their own languages and translate the relevant information into English. If you plan to give your students class time to work on the itinerary, you'll need to ask them beforehand to bring in their travel guides for the lesson. If your students have access to the Internet, they could also use this as a source of information.

Since it takes time to plan such a trip, you may want to give the students the opportunity to begin their work in class and then give them a few days to work on their itineraries at home before bringing them to class. (You may also choose to shorten the trip to one week.) It is helpful if the students focus their itineraries on one major city and its environs. Once the itineraries have been completed, have the students work in pairs for ten minutes asking one another about their trips. You can then have students get with a new partner to find out about another person's trip.

2.9c. Application

> Travel log; L, S, R, W; i & iii+ & iiiii
> 15+ minutes/Homework

To develop this stage of the lesson into a writing activity, you can have the students write a travel log based upon their itineraries. Be sure to tell them that they do not need to account for every day in the trip but that they should describe the main events. Encourage the students to use their imaginations to describe what happened at a given place. If possible, make copies of the travel logs and share them with the students or have them share their itineraries orally in groups. As a class, discuss which trips students would like to go on (see activity 3.6 for adapting this activity to the use of the future tense).

2.10. The Simple Past and Past Progressive: History

2.10a. Presentation

> Historical time line; L, S, R; iii+
> Materials included
> 15–20 minutes/Homework

This extended lesson brings a bit of world history into a grammar class. Explain to the students that you are going to discuss a historical time line in periods of one hundred years (see Appendix 2.10a for a copy of this time line). Most of the items in this time line focus on European culture. You may want to make a time line that focuses on the historical heritage shared by your students. Give the students the opportunity to read through the time line in groups of three and to discuss any new vocabulary among themselves and then as a class. Or, to save class time, give the students the opportunity to review the time line for homework. Then you can discuss their questions during the next lesson.

2.10b. Practice

> Historical clock; L, S, R; ii
> 15 minutes

Tell the students that they should think of each century as representing one hour on a clock starting at midnight representing the year A.D. 1. In pairs, they can take turns asking one another what happened at a given hour. A student can ask his or her partner what happened at the various hours between 12:00 in the morning and 12:00 in the afternoon. The students will need to match up the time with the appropriate date on the time line. Since some of the events took place just before or after the turn of a given century, a student might ask, "What happened just before 2:00 in the afternoon?" or "What happened just after 8:00 in the evening?" The students will also have to decide whether the simple past, past progressive, or passive voice works best with the event described in the time line. Have the students change partners after about seven minutes.

2.10c. Application

Research; W; i & iii+ & iiiii
Homework/15 minutes

Have the students research other events to add to the time line. (If your students have access to the Internet, they can do a search under "history" to find a wide selection of topics related to historical events.) They can also add times to the clock. These can then be shared with the class. You could also have groups of students work on a time line together. In this case, you could suggest that each group work on a theme such as inventions or developments in architecture, music, or science and/or that each group focus on a specific period in history. Remind the students to use the present tense when writing information on the time line so that their classmates will be able to practice changing the verbs into the past tense when they ask one another questions about the time line. If the students choose to work on events which took place prior to A.D. 1, you may want to remind them that the larger the number, the further back in time the event occurred.

If your students have access to information about the development of the earth and life on the planet, it's also interesting to cover larger spans of time on the historical clock with one hour representing a thousand years. Or, alternatively, you could have the students focus on more recent history, making sixty years equivalent to one hour. So, the 1900s would begin at 12:00, five after 12:00 would be 1905, ten after 12:00 would represent 1910, etc.

2.11. The Simple Past: Poem

2.11a. Presentation

Word families; L, S, R, W; i & ii & iiiii
10–15 minutes

To introduce the poem "A Poison Tree" by the English poet William Blake (1757–1827), write the following set of words on the board.

    poison
    angry
    wrath
    foe

fears

tears

deceitful

wiles

death

Read the words aloud to the students and have them repeat each one after you. Then give them a few minutes to look up any new words in their dictionaries. Also, they should note down the part of speech for each word. Discuss any vocabulary questions as a class. Once the students are familiar with the words, ask them what the words share in common. The students will probably notice that they are all negative. Tell the students that they are going to read a poem by the English poet William Blake (1757–1827) called "A Poison Tree" and that most of these words appear in the poem.

Based on this selection of words, have them write a few sentences about what they think the poem might be about. They can then share their ideas in pairs and as a class. Some students may make the association between the poison tree and the allusion to the tree of knowledge in the creation story found in the book of Genesis, one of the thirty-nine books of the Jewish Bible. In Genesis, God creates the Garden of Eden for the first man and woman, Adam and Eve, but he tells them not to eat of the fruit from the Tree of Knowledge or else they will experience evil and death. Unfortunately, they are tempted to eat of the fruit and experience evil and death as a result. If you refer to this creation story, you may want to have the students share other creation stories with which they are familiar.

At this point, ask the students to write words that are opposite in meaning to the words listed such as

poison (n.)	medicine
angry (adj.)	happy
wrath (n.)	happiness
foe (n.)	friend
fears (n.)	confidence/courage/bravery
tears (n.)	smiles
deceitful (adj.)	truthful/honest
wiles (n.)	truthfulness/honesty
death (n.)	life

Explain that William Blake wrote two books of poems, the *Songs of Innocence* (1789) and *Songs of Experience* (1794). The poems in both books are told from a child's point of view: in the *Songs of Innocence*, the child portrays the world as being good whereas in *Songs of Experience*, the child portrays the bad things in the world. Ask the students to identify which list of words written on the board could be associated with *Songs of Innocence* and which could be associated with *Songs of Experience.*

2.11b. Practice

> Sequencing; R, W; i & iii+
> Materials included
> 20 minutes

Write up the first stanza of the poem on the board (or project it on an overhead screen). Read it for the students. Then ask them to rewrite the first stanza in prose form using their own words. For example:

STANZA 1

> I was angry with my friend:
> I told my wrath, my wrath did end.
> I was angry with my foe:
> I told it not, my wrath did grow.

Prose version

> I was angry with my friend and I told her about it. After that, I wasn't angry anymore. But, when I was angry with my enemy, I didn't tell her about it and I got even angrier.

Have small groups of students share what they've written and ask each group to read one version for the class.

Explain that Blake compares the speaker's growing anger to a growing poison tree. Based on this information, ask the groups to put the poem's remaining three stanzas in the correct order. (A jumbled copy of the poem can be found in Appendix 2.11b. You can give the students the work sheet or cut out the stanzas and have each group work together to reorder the poems.) The correct order is as follows.

Stanza 2 is c
Stanza 3 is b
Stanza 4 is a

To help your students determine the correct order of the stanzas, ask them to think about the answers to the questions that follow the jumble of stanzas. The key to the questions is as follows.

1. What did the speaker's enemy see shining on the tree?
    She or he saw the growing fruit.
2. What did the enemy want?
    She or he wanted to take the fruit.
3. Who stole into the garden? When? Why?
    The enemy stole into the garden at night to steal the fruit because it was the speaker's fruit.
4. What happened to the speaker's enemy? Why? How did the speaker feel about this?
    The speaker's enemy died because she or he ate the poisoned fruit. The speaker felt glad about it.
5. Identify what *it* refers to each time it is used.
    Stanza 1: *It* refers to the speaker's anger.
    Stanza 2 (c): The first and second *it* refer to the poison tree.
    Stanza 3 (b): The first and second *it* refer to the poison tree. The third and fourth *it* refer to the tree's fruit.
6. Which verb in the poem is written in the present tense? Why?
    The verb *see* because the speaker is thinking of the morning in the present tense and/or because Blake needed a word to rhyme with *tree.*
7. How does the punctuation used in stanzas 3 and 4 help you to order them?
    Stanza 3 does not end with a full stop, and the sentence continues in stanza 4.

2.11c. Application

> **Prose writing; L, S, W; i & iiiii**
> **15+ minutes/Homework**

Discuss the students' reactions to the poem. What do they think about the speaker? Have they ever been angry and not told someone about it? What was the result? How do they think an enemy should be treated? You may prefer to have students write out their private responses to the poem rather than discussing them publicly since some students may feel uncomfortable sharing such personal experiences with the class.

In the poem, Blake uses poetic language to describe how the poison tree grows, and, in fact, the poison tree itself is a metaphor for the speaker's growing anger and hate. Based on "A Poison Tree," have the students write a paragraph in which they describe what could have actually happened in a real-life situation. Encourage the students to use their imaginations to determine how the ideas in the poem might actually be experienced in everyday life. The students can relate the ideas in the poem to themselves or to other situations in life—particularly those related to warfare and politics—when people have tricked their enemies. If you are teaching in a politically sensitive environment, use your discretion when assigning the final application activity.

For a more positive contrast to this poem, see extended lessons 1.11 and 3.11. You can also have the students read one of Blake's poems from his *Songs of Innocence.*

Appendix 2.1. Fables

The Wind and the Sun

The wind and the sun were arguing about who was the stronger.

Suddenly they saw a man walking on the road, and the wind said,

"I see a way to end our argument."

"Whichever of us can make that man take off his coat is the stronger."

But the harder he blew, the more closely the man held his coat to him.

The wind finally gave up trying.

Then the sun came out and shone upon the man, who soon became hot and took off his coat.

The Dog and the Reflection

It happened that a dog had a big piece of meat and was carrying it home in his mouth to eat.

Now, on his way home, he had to cross a log lying across a stream.

As he crossed the stream, he looked down and saw his own image reflected in the water.

Thinking it was another dog with another piece of meat, he made up his mind to get the meat.

So, he tried to bite at the reflection in the water.

But, as he opened his mouth, his piece of meat fell out and dropped into the water.

It was never seen again.

Appendix 2.2. Time Lines

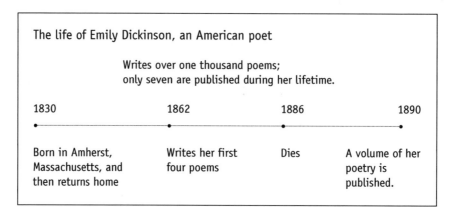

The life of Emily Dickinson, an American poet

Writes over one thousand poems;
only seven are published during her lifetime.

1830	1862	1886	1890
Born in Amherst, Massachusetts, and then returns home	Writes her first four poems	Dies	A volume of her poetry is published.

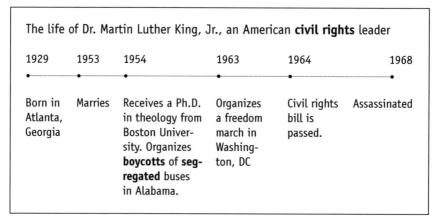

The life of Dr. Martin Luther King, Jr., an American **civil rights** leader

1929	1953	1954	1963	1964	1968
Born in Atlanta, Georgia	Marries	Receives a Ph.D. in theology from Boston University. Organizes **boycotts** of **segregated** buses in Alabama.	Organizes a freedom march in Washington, DC	Civil rights bill is passed.	Assassinated

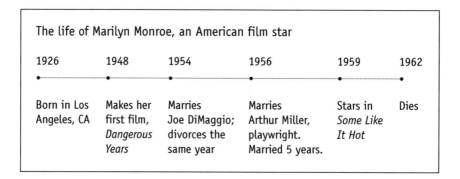

The life of Marilyn Monroe, an American film star

1926	1948	1954	1956	1959	1962
Born in Los Angeles, CA	Makes her first film, *Dangerous Years*	Marries Joe DiMaggio; divorces the same year	Marries Arthur Miller, playwright. Married 5 years.	Stars in *Some Like It Hot*	Dies

© 1999 University of Michigan Press

---

civil rights: the rights a person has as a human being and as a member of a civil society
boycott: a person refuses to use a service or product
segregated: The buses were segregated. This means that members from different races could not sit together. In Alabama, the Blacks were made to sit in the back of the bus.

Appendix 2.4. Chart

Name_____

Record of When I Checked the Time and What I Was Doing Then

Time	Activity

Appendix 2.6. Trends

Illustrations from "Lifestyles," in *Interactions II: A Reading Skills Book,* 3rd edition, edited by Elaine Kirn and Pamela Hartmann. Copyright © 1996, 1990, 1985. Reprinted by permission of The McGraw-Hill Companies.

Appendix 2.7a. *Used To*

Appendix 2.7b. *Used To*

Name(s)_____

Appendix 2.9a, Option One. Itinerary

August

Sun. 1	Mon. 2	Tues. 3	Wed. 4	Thurs. 5	Fri. 6	Sat. 7
Arrive in London late afternoon Take a walk along the Thames Go out to a pub	Visit the British Museum Explore the Bloomsbury area of city Tour the Tower of London and the bridge	Tour Buckingham Palace High tea at the Ritz Westminster Abbey	Spend a few hours at the Victoria and Albert Museum Explore Hyde Park Stop by the National History Museum	Visit the National Gallery and explore Trafalgar Square Dancing in the evening at Iceni's	Excursion to Windsor Castle Attend the opera at the Royal Opera House	Weekend trip to Oxford Visit Christ's Church, University College, and the Botanical Gardens
Sun. 8	**Mon. 9**	**Tues. 10**	**Wed. 11**	**Thurs. 12**	**Fri. 13**	**Sat. 14**
Day trip to Stratford-upon-Avon Pay respects at Shakespeare's grave Watch the Royal Shakespeare Company Return late to Oxford	Explore Oxford some more Return to London in the late afternoon Evening out	Day excursion to Dover Visit Dover castle See the white cliffs of Dover	Sleep in Shopping all day!	Day excursion to Salisbury Visit the Salisbury Cathedral and Stonehenge	Pack Visit the Tate Gallery Royal Albert Hall concert in the evening	Return home

Appendix 2.9a, Option Two. Itinerary

Name(s)_____

August

Sun. 1	Mon. 2	Tues. 3	Wed. 4	Thurs. 5	Fri. 6	Sat. 7
Sun. 8	Mon. 9	Tues. 10	Wed. 11	Thurs. 12	Fri. 13	Sat. 14

Appendix 2.10a. Time Line

A.D. 1 (anno Domini—in the year of our Lord)
The birth of Christ is traditionally believed to be A.D. 1, though scholars list his birth date as A.D. 4 in Bethlehem, a town in the Roman Empire. He is believed to have been **crucified** in 30 A.D. His followers were **persecuted** for believing that Christ was the son of God and that he rose from the dead. Eventually, Christianity, the religion named after Christ, became an important religion in Europe, the Americas, and parts of Asia.

A.D. 100
Golden Age of the Roman Empire. The emperor Marcus Aurelius (161–80) writes his *Meditations,* a book that outlines his **moral philosophy**. He also reforms the legal system to make it fairer and gives more rights to slaves. He starts many social services for the poor such as schools, hospitals, and **orphanages.**

A.D. 200
Development of the so-called Silk Road from China through the Gobi Desert and Central Asia. Traders from Rome take wool, silver, and gold to China. From China, they bring back silk, porcelain, and tea.

A.D. 300
Rule of Constantine the Great in Rome from 306 to 337. He moves the capital of the empire from Rome to Constantinople, which is now Istanbul, the modern day capital city of Turkey. He is known for ending the persecution of Christians in the Roman Empire.

A.D. 400
Nomadic tribes begin to invade Italy. A Germanic tribe called the Goths invades Rome in 410. As the Roman Empire collapses, the Dark Ages (450–1000) begin.

---

crucified: nailed to a cross until dead
persecuted: treated unfairly, sometimes put in prison or killed for their beliefs
moral philosophy: beliefs about how to live a good life
orphanages: homes for children whose parents are no longer living or who can no longer take care of them
nomadic tribes: small groups of people who move from place to place

A.D. 500

In Constantinople, the emperor Justinian I orders the construction of the Hagia Sophia (532–62). The name Hagia Sophia means *the Church of Holy Wisdom*. The cathedral has been a Christian church and a **Muslim mosque** at different times in its history. At present, it is a museum.

A.D. 600

Muhammad, the prophet of Islam, is born in Mecca (ca. 570–632). In 622 he leaves Mecca for Medina to escape his enemies. This event marks the beginning of the Islamic calendar. Muhammad overcomes his enemies and becomes a powerful ruler and religious leader in Arabia. He lays the foundation for the Islamic empire.

A.D. 700

In Europe, the **Roman chant** is renamed the Gregorian chant in honor of Saint Gregory II (669–731), who was **pope** from 715–31. The Gregorian chant was a popular religious form of music from the fifth to the seventh century.

A.D. 800

Charlemagne (742–814) comes to power as a king of the Franks (768–814). He becomes one of the most powerful kings of the Middle Ages. His rule is known for bringing together Germanic, Roman, and Christian traditions.

The English king, Alfred the Great (849–99) comes to power in 871. He is known for laying the foundation that made England one country. He also makes his court a center of learning.

A.D. 900

Al-Razi, a Muslim physician and writer (ca. 865–935), writes a twenty-volume medical encyclopedia that brings together traditions in medicine from Greece, Syria, and Arabia. His work influences medical thought during the Middle Ages in both Islamic and European regions.

Muslim: a person who follows the religion of Islam
mosque: a place where Muslims worship Allah, their name for God
Roman chant: a religious song sung without the use of musical instruments
pope: the leader of the Catholic Church

A.D. 1000

Leif Eriksson sets up a Viking outpost in North America that he calls Vinland. In 1963, remains of a Viking-like outpost were found in New-foundland, and this site is believed to be Eriksson's settlement.

A.D. 1100

In 1154, work begins on the building of the Chartres Cathedral in France. In the United States, Native Americans in what is now central Arizona build magnificent **cliff dwellings** for protection. Remains of these dwellings can be seen in **Casa Grande** National Monument.

A.D. 1200

Marco Polo (1254–1324) travels on the Silk Road with his father in 1260 in order to trade with Asian peoples. It takes them three years to get to China, and they stay in Asia for nine years. Later, Polo writes *The Travels of Marco Polo*, which gives many Europeans their first picture of life in Asia.

---

cliff dwellings: villages built on high rock ledges
Casa Grande: Spanish for *Large House*. A national park is an area of land that is protected from development.

Appendix 2.11b. Poem   Name(s)_____

William Blake (1757–1827)

A POISON TREE

STANZA 1

> I was angry with my friend:
> I told my wrath, my wrath did end.
> I was angry with my foe:
> I told it not, my wrath did grow.

Put these three additional stanzas from Blake's "The Poison Tree" into their correct order. Write the number 2, 3, or 4 in the blanks to show the order in which these three stanzas follow stanza 1.

STANZA a __

> And into the garden **stole**
> When the **night veiled the pole:**
> And in the morning glad I see
> My foe **outstretched** beneath the tree.

STANZA b __

> And it grew both day and night,
> Till it bore an apple bright;
> And my foe **beheld** it shine,
> And he knew that it was mine,

STANZA c __

> And I **water'd** it with my fears,
> Night and morning with my tears;
> And I **sunn'd** it with my smiles,
> And with soft deceitful wiles.

The poem "A Poison Tree" (presented here in jumbled order as part of the exercise) is in the public domain. Questions © 1999 University of Michigan.

---

stole into: came in secretly
night veiled the pole: the dark night hid the tree trunk
outstretched: lying on the ground
beheld: saw
watered: Gave the tree water. In this poem, the water is likened to the speaker's fears.
sunned: Gave the tree sunshine. In this poem, the sunshine is likened to the speaker's false smiles.

Name(s)_____

Questions for Poem

To help you order the stanzas, think about the answers to the following questions.

1. What did the speaker's enemy see shining on the tree?

2. What did the enemy want?

3. Who stole into the garden? When? Why?

4. What happened to the speaker's enemy? Why? How did the speaker feel about this?

5. Identify what *it* refers to each time it is used:

   Stanza 1:

   Stanza 2:

   Stanza 3:

6. Which verb in the poem is written in the present tense? Why?

7. How does the punctuation used in stanzas 3 and 4 help you to order them?

Chapter 3

The Future Tense

Itemized Reference List

Skill Areas		Group Work	
Listening	L	Individual	i
Speaking	S	Pair	ii
Reading	R	Small Group	iii+
Writing	W	Class	iiiii

Structure		Activity	Skills	Groups	Appendix
Supplementary Activities					
3.1.	*Be Going to* and *Will*	Prediction	L, S, W	ii	102
3.2.	*Going to*	Second identity	L, S, W	i & iii+ & iiiii	103
3.3.	Expressing the Future in *If* Clauses	Making choices	L, S	i & ii & iiiii	104
3.4.	Expressing the Future	Nostradamus	L, S, W	i & iii+ & iiiii	105
3.5.	Simple Future and Future Progressive	Time focus	L, S	ii	
3.6.	Expressing Future Plans	Itinerary	L, S, W	ii & iii+ & iiiii	
3.7.	Review of the Past, Present, and Future Tenses	Letters	W	i	106
Extended Lessons					
3.8.	Expressing Future Time in *If* Clauses: Poem				
3.8a.	Presentation	Making a choice	L, S	iiiii	
3.8b.	Practice	Discourse analysis	R	i or iii+	107
3.8c.	Application	Personalization	W	i	
3.9.	Expressing the Future and *Yes/No* Questions: Poem				
3.9a.	Presentation	Question formation	L, S	iiiii	
3.9b.	Practice: Option One	Sentence completion	W	i & ii & iiiii	108
3.9b.	Practice: Option Two	Sentence completion	W	i & ii & iiiii	109
3.9c.	Application	Travel poem	R, W	i & ii & iiiii	110
3.10.	Expressing *If I Ever* Clauses: Song/Personalization				
3.10a.	Presentation	Word analysis	L, S	iiiii	
3.10b.	Practice	Sentence completion	L, S, W	i & iii+ & iiiii	
3.10c.	Application: Option One	Cloze and/or journal	L, S, R, W	i & ii & iiiii	
3.10c.	Application: Option Two	Journal and/or poem	W	i	
3.10c.	Application: Option Three	Biography (Past tense)	L, S, R, W	i & iiiii	111
3.11.	Expressing Future Time: Speech				
3.11a.	Presentation	Word association	W	iii+ & iiiii	117
3.11b.	Practice	Cloze	L, S	i & iiiii	
3.11c.	Application	Personalization	W	i & iiiii	

Supplementary Activities

3.1. *Be Going to* and *Will*

> **Prediction; L, S, W; ii**
> **Materials included**

To practice the use of *is going to,* have students predict a person's future profession based on information about his or her interests and studies. Point out that the use of *going to* suggests that the person is probably planning to do something specific in the future. For example, consider the following information about Jean Smith.

> Jean Smith (15 years old)
> • studies guitar
> • has a great voice
> • collects rock 'n' roll music
> • writes music

When you present the information to the class, take on the persona of the person who is being described. So, you might say the following.

> Hi, I'm Jean Smith. I'm really into music. I study guitar, and I have a great voice. I also write music. I have a great collection of rock 'n' roll music. What do you think I'm going to be in the future?

Students should answer the question using the third-person point of view as in "You're going to be a rock musician."

Based on the information given, you could also encourage the students to use *will* to come up with assertions about the person whose future is being described. In this case, the students should use *will* to say what else they think or guess will probably happen to this person in the future: "You'll be famous. You'll be a great rock musician."

Once you have modeled this activity for the students, have them use the situations found in Appendix 3.1 as the basis for their predictions. However, you may want to create materials that are more culturally relevant to your students. In pairs, one student should present the information using the first-person point of view, and the other student should make the prediction. Once the students are comfortable with the format of the activity, ask them to write up similar information that you can then use for practice in class.

3.2. *Going to*

> **Second identity; L, S, W; i & iii+ & iiiii**
> **Materials included**

If you have completed activities 1.2, 1.3, or 2.2 with the students, refer to the well-known people the students previously discussed to complete this activity. Otherwise, you'll need to make sure that the students have some background information about the people referred to in the lesson.

Then give each student a slip of paper with the name of a famous person with whom the class is familiar. Arrange it so that two or three people have the same person. Give the students time to respond in writing to the following prompt that can be written up on the board or projected on a screen.

> Imagine that you are _____, but that you are only ten years old. Write a few sentences in which you tell what you are going to be when you grow up and what you are going to do in your life. You can also describe how you think you will probably act and look and what people will think about you.

After the class has had time to write out their responses, have the students who have written about the same person get into groups to share their responses. If students learn something new from their classmates, they can add this information to what they have written. Then give the students the opportunity to walk around the room asking people who weren't in their group, "Who are you?" and "What are you going to do when you grow up?" Students can use the chart provided in Appendix 3.2 to record the information. After the students have had some time to compile information, have the class discuss the people they have met and the things they have learned about a given person's future.

3.3. Expressing the Future in *If* Clauses

> **Making choices; L, S; i & ii & iiiii**
> **Materials included**

Present the students with situations where there are two alternative choices. Ask students what will happen if either choice is decided upon. The students should respond imaginatively to the prompts using an *if* clause to express future time. As an example, consider the following prompt.

1. You are thinking about taking a two-week vacation from school or work.
    A. What will happen if you take a vacation?
    B. What will happen if you don't take a vacation?

Students might respond to A and B as follows.

A. If I take a vacation, I will get to relax and I will see another country.
B. If I don't take a vacation, I won't miss work and my boss will be happy.

If the students are able to use modals such as *could* and *might* to express a future possibility, have them use these forms as well. They should be sure to use *if* clauses to express a future result. For sample situations, refer to Appendix 3.3. Give the students time in class or as homework to prepare their responses before they share them in pairs. You can also have the students devise their own situations that can then be used in class. Suggest that the students use choices that they may actually have to make in the future. If you would like to develop this idea into an extended lesson, refer to lesson 3.8.

3.4. Expressing the Future

> **Nostradamus; L, S, W; i & iii+ & iiiii**
> **Materials included**

To introduce this activity, ask the students what they know about a man named Nostradamus who lived from A.D. 1503 to 1566. In the course of the discussion, make sure the students understand that Nostradamus was a French doctor and an astrologer who was known for his ability to predict the future. He wrote two books, *Prophecies* and *Centuries,* in which he predicted future events and inventions. Here is a short list of some of the predictions Nostradamus made that apparently came true.

1. The rule of Queen Elizabeth I in England
2. The rule of Napoleon in France
3. The invention of the submarine
4. The development of the nuclear bomb

However, when Nostradamus made his predictions, he did not always have the words to describe what he wanted to predict so he had to use descriptions and explanations to give people an understanding of what he meant. For example, he once had a vision of a submarine, but, since the submarine did not yet exist, he did not have a word for it and so described it as "an iron fish enclosing men, usually traveling with a warlike intent."

Tell your students to imagine that they are living in the 1500s. Explain to them that you are going to describe an invention or a technology that does not yet exist. From your description, the students should try to guess what the discovery is. For example, of the computer you could say, "It looks like a box with many buttons. It can do calculations rapidly." With the class, brainstorm a list of inventions and technological developments that have significantly impacted modern life in both rural and urban areas. Ask each student to choose one item to write about or give each student an item from the list found in Appendix 3.4. Remind the students that like Nostradamus they are making a prediction about how this discovery will change society, so they will need to write using the future tense. Also, they should think of creative ways to describe the technology or invention. Then, as a class, or in groups of three or more, students can read out their clues while the other students try to guess what invention or technology is being described.

3.5. Simple Future and Future Progressive

> **Time focus; L, S; ii**
> **Materials included**

If you have already done activity 1.6 with the students, then simply review the time zones. If not, then follow the steps outlined in the activity. Once the students are comfortable expressing the time in different parts of the world using the present and present progressive tenses, have them switch to the future tense. They will need to add time expressions to their questions such as

In three hours, what will people in Paris be doing?
In five hours, what will happen in Moscow?

As with activity 1.6, have the students try to come up with activities and events that actually pertain to a given place.

3.6. Expressing Future Plans

> **Itinerary; L, S, W; ii & iii+ & iiiii**
> **Materials included**

If you have previously done extended lesson 2.9, then refer to the itinerary that you used for this lesson (see Appendix 2.9a for a sample itinerary). If you have not yet done this lesson, first follow the steps outlined in activity 2.9a. When students ask one another questions about their trips, in pairs or in small groups, have them use the future tense. Tell them to imagine that it is the day before their classmate will go on the trip. Before students ask one another questions, you may need to review time expressions and verbs such as *plan, intend, expect,* and *hope* that are associated with the future tense. After the students have discussed their trips, have them write a short description of what they are planning to do during their holidays.

3.7. Review of the Past, Present, and Future Tenses

> **Letters; W; i**
> **Materials included**

Ask the students to write a letter in which they imagine that they are on a holiday in a beautiful city, say, for example, Paris, and are sitting at an outdoor café writing a letter to their family, a friend, or a pen pal. Direct the students to begin the letter with the time expression *now.* In the letter, students should try to use each of the following time expressions.

- today
- yesterday
- recently (in British English, *recently* is more commonly used with the present perfect)
- this morning/afternoon/evening
- at the moment
- tomorrow
- a _____ ago
- _____ ago
- on + a date (on April 5th)
- just
- Frequency adverbs (see activity 1.2)

(After the students have learned time expressions associated with the present perfect forms such as *yet, already, recently, for a long time,* and *since,* add these to the list of time expressions.) You can give the students the following outline to help them write their letters.

> Paragraph 1: Describe where you are and what is happening around you.
> Paragraph 2: Describe some of the things you did a few days ago.
> Paragraph 3: Describe what you plan to do in the near future.

Encourage the students to use their imaginations to make their letters more interesting. If the students have already completed activity 3.6 or extended lesson 2.9, they can refer to their itineraries for ideas. If your students have not completed these activities or have not had opportunities to travel, suggest that they imagine that they are writing the letter during a break at school.

To make this activity more challenging, you can ask the students to write a problem/solution letter using the time expressions already listed in this activity. They can choose to focus on a problem in their own communities or in another part of the world. If possible, have the students actually address their letters to someone who has the power to help solve the problem. If you choose to have the students write this letter, be sure that they are already familiar with using *if* clauses to express future situations. (If your students are familiar with modals have them also offer solutions to the problem using modals.) Use the outline in Appendix 3.7 to help the students organize their letters.

Extended Lessons

3.8. Expressing Future Time in *If* Clauses: Poem

3.8a. Presentation

> Making a choice; L, S; iiiii
> 10 minutes

As a way to introduce this lesson, do activity 3.3 first. Then explain to the students that they will be reading the poem "The Road Not Taken" by the American poet, Robert Frost (1874–1963). Ask the students to use their imaginations to answer the following questions.

1. Based on the title "The Road Not Taken," what do you think the poem is going to be about?
2. If you were walking or driving on a dirt road in the countryside, and you came to a fork in the road, would you take the road that looked like more or fewer people had used it? Why?

Make sure the students understand that in this poem when the speaker comes to a fork in the road, he must decide whether he should take the road to the left or to the right. We don't know much about the speaker, and we aren't told which direction the speaker went, but we do know he took the road that looked as if fewer people had traveled on it. We also don't know what happened to the speaker as a result of this decision.

Before the students read the poem, you may want to preteach some of the key words found in the text.

diverged
undergrowth
trodden
hence
grassy
to wear on something
a bend in the road

3.8b. Practice

> **Discourse analysis; R; i or iii+**
> **Materials included**
> **20 minutes**

In Appendix 3.8b, you will find a jumbled copy of the poem. Either give the students the handout and have them number the stanzas in the correct order or cut the stanzas out and ask the students to put them in the correct order. Students can work on this task alone or in small groups. The correct order is as follows.

1. Stanza b
2. Stanza d
3. Stanza a
4. Stanza c

To help the students determine the sequence of the stanzas, have them think about the answers to the following questions that you can write up on the board or display using an overhead projector. The key to the answers is as follows.

1. How long ago do you think the speaker came to the fork in the road?
   Maybe a short time ago, a few months or a few years. But not for a very long time because he still has "ages and ages" to live.
2. When will the speaker think about the decision he made at the fork in the road?
   Sometime far in the future—"ages and ages hence."

You might also want to help the students by telling them the correct position of one of the stanzas before they begin ordering them.

Once the students have had some time to order the stanzas, discuss the results as a class. Then share the original version of the poem with the students. For a writing activity, you could then have the students rewrite the poem in prose form. So, for the first stanza a student might say or write:

> When I was walking in the woods, I came to a fork in the road. I was sorry I couldn't take both roads. I thought about the best road to take. I looked down the roads as far as I could.

Discuss the paraphrases as a class.

3.8c. Application

> Personalization; W; i
> 20 minutes/Homework

Ask each student to write about a decision he or she made in the past and how it changed his or her life. Then ask them to write about a decision that they will have to make in the future. Direct the students to use *if* clauses with future time as is shown in activity 3.3. If some students do not feel comfortable writing such personal information, ask them to write about decisions that other people—real or fictional—will have to make. Or suggest that the students write about actual decisions political leaders must make and what the results will be or could possibly be. Then they can ask one another what will or won't happen as a result of the choice that will be made.

If you are teaching in a country where the political situation is particularly sensitive, you may want to forgo this last option or change the context to a less volatile one.

3.9. Expressing the Future and *Yes/No* Questions: Poem

3.9a. Presentation

> **Question formation; L, S; iiiii**
> **10 minutes**

This lesson is based on the poem "Uphill" written by Christine Rossetti (1839–94), an English poet. The author uses a style of English common to the 1800s; as a result, some of the expressions used in the poem may sound unfamiliar to your students. Throughout the stages of the lesson, the more archaic expressions are also written in their modern equivalents to make the materials more accessible to your students. If you think that your students will be confused by the style of English used in this poem, then I would advise choosing another activity. However, you may find that your students find the contrast interesting. Also, it is helpful for students to be aware that the English language has changed throughout the centuries and that it is in fact changing now.

Should you decide to use this poem, have the students imagine that they are in London and that they are preparing to travel on foot to a town in the English countryside. Explain that they will be walking quite a distance and that they would like to arrive in the town by nightfall. They are not sure whether or not there will be a place to stay the night. Together, think of some questions they might have about the journey if they were to meet someone from the town before setting out. Here are some possible questions. (*Note:* Encourage the students to include a few yes/no questions.)

- How long does it take to get there?
- Are there rooms available for rent? For how much?
- Is it hard to find an inn or a hotel?
- Are people friendly there?
- Who will I meet there?

Take this opportunity to preteach the following vocabulary.

a winding road
a wayfarer
travel-sore
the sum
an inn

3.9b. Practice

> Sentence completion; W; i & ii & iiiii
> Materials included
> 15–20 minutes

Give the students the questions from the poem "Uphill." Ask them to write in their responses to the speaker's questions (see Appendix 3.9b, Option One [p. 108], for a copy of this exercise). Then have them share their answers in pairs and as a class. Before the students write out their responses, take a minute to discuss any vocabulary questions the students might have.

As an alternative approach, you can give the students the answers and have them write questions that they think are appropriate (see Appendix 3.9b, Option Two [p. 109]). Or, you could choose to give half of the class the answers and half the questions!

3.9c. Application

> Travel poem; R, W; i & ii & iiiii
> Materials included
> 15–20 minutes/Homework

Share the final version of the poem with the students (see Appendix 3.9c for a copy of the poem). In pairs, have the students read it aloud with one person

---

a wayfarer: someone who is on a journey, usually on foot

reading the questions and the other the answers. Then read the poem as a class with half the students reading the questions and the other half responding.

Assuming that the person asking the question is on a journey, ask the students which question and answer seems out of place. Some may notice that line 14 refers to labor and wages. How does this information change the poem? What is the speaker of the poem looking for besides a place to stay? Why is the poem entitled "Uphill"? Students might notice that the title "Uphill" can refer not only to the journey described by the wayfarer but also to the uphill effort a person makes to live life successfully. At this point in the lesson, you may want to share the idiomatic expression *an up-hill battle* with the students and have them discuss how this expression might relate to the poem. The students should notice that the speaker of the poem is probably looking for work and is not on holidays.

As homework, give your students the opportunity to try writing their own "poem." Have them follow the same format that Rossetti has used: a series of *yes/no* questions followed by answers. The students may choose a similar or different topic to write about. For topic ideas, refer to the situations listed in Appendix 1.1.

You can also have students find the rhyming words in the poem and ask them to mark each set of rhyming words with an uppercase letter from the alphabet beginning with A, and so on. The pattern they should find is ABAB/CDCD/EFEF/GHGH. Suggest that the students try to create a similar pattern of rhyme but be sure to tell them that they don't have to follow the original rhyming pattern exactly, nor do they need to have as many stanzas. To help the students organize their poems, you can also point out that Rossetti has focused on a related set of questions in each stanza.

Stanza 1: Questions about the journey
Stanza 2: Questions about lodgings
Stanza 3: Questions about who the traveler will meet
Stanza 4: Questions about finding comfort at the journey's end

If your students are uncomfortable writing poetry, simply have them write a series of questions and answers. Ask them to include some yes/no questions in the sequence.

3.10. Expressing *If I Ever* Clauses: Song/Personalization

3.10a. Presentation

> Word analysis; L, S; iiiii
> 10 minutes

Write the verb *to lose* on the board. Ask the students what meanings this verb can have as in *to lose a game, to lose your wallet, to lose your way*. Then discuss what *to lose* might mean in the following phrases.

> to lose one's hands
> to lose one's eyes
> to lose one's legs
> to lose one's ears
> to lose one's mouth

You can point out to the students that *to lose* in these phrases can mean *to lose the ability to be able to use something*. Discuss the vocabulary that can be associated with the loss of each feature. For example, for the loss of one's eyes, you can elicit and/or preteach the following: *to be blind, a guide dog, darkness, braille*. And, for the loss of hearing, students might come up with *to be deaf, sign language, silence,* and *hearing aid*. The idea is simply to come up with related vocabulary terms for each item in the list.

3.10b. Practice

> Sentence completion; L, S, W; i & iii+ & iiiii
> 15–20 minutes

Then, write the *if* clauses found below on the board and ask the students to finish the sentences using *won't* after the clause. You can point out that the simple future is used to show what a person really will or won't do if something ever happens. The use of *if* with the future tense personalizes the experience. (If your students are already familiar with the use of *if* to express an unreal situation, you might want to explain that the speaker could have chosen to say, "If I ever lose my hands, I wouldn't be able to work," but that the use of this tense depersonalizes the experience, making it seem like it couldn't really happen to the speaker. Of course, this is a rather fine distinction and might be confusing to your students, so only bring it up if someone asks about it or if you think it would be of interest to the students.) Here are the sentences the students should complete.

> If I ever lose my hands, I won't . . .
> If I ever lose my eyes, I won't . . .
> If I ever lose my legs, I won't . . .
> If I ever lose my mouth, I won't . . .
> If I ever lose my ears, I won't . . .

Have the students share their responses in groups of three or more and then again as a class. Assuming that most students will focus on the negative results of the *if* clause, ask them to reconsider their completion of the sentences by finishing the sentences using *I won't have to.*

> If I ever lose my hands, I won't have to . . .
> If I ever lose my eyes, I won't have to . . .
> If I ever lose my legs, I won't have to . . .
> If I ever lose my mouth, I won't have to . . .
> If I ever lose my ears, I won't have to . . .

3.10c. Application

Ideally, the presentation and practice stages should be followed by having students listen to the song "Moonshadow" by Cat Stevens (© 1989 A&M Records). If you have access to the song, then you can complete all of the options provided in this stage of the lesson. If you are unable to obtain a copy of the song, simply skip Option One and have the students complete Option Two. With or without the song lyrics, Option Three provides students with a thought-provoking way to consider the themes raised by the presentation and practice stages of the lesson.

Option One

> **Cloze and/or journal; L, S, R, W; i & ii & iiiii**
> **20+ minutes**

For this option, you will need to bring in a recording of the song "Moonshadow" by Cat Stevens. Explain to the students that they will be listening to a song in which the singer thinks about how the loss of his hands, eyes, legs, mouth, and ears might affect his life. Make a cloze exercise in which you leave off the part of the sentence that follows the *if* clause. Before the students actually listen to the song and complete the cloze, give them the opportunity to read through the passage and to discuss any new vocabulary terms. Play the song and ask the students to fill in the blanks as they listen. Let the students compare their answers and play the song through again. Then share the correct responses with the students. You can have the students do a choral reading in which one half of the class reads the dependent *if* clauses and the other half of the class reads the independent clauses that express a future action. Students may also want to discuss the speaker's attitude based on the way he has completed the *if* clauses. The following questions will help to lead into such a discussion.

1. What does the speaker say is following him?
   [A moonshadow]
2. What is a *moonshadow?*
   [The shadows cast by the moon. Time.] (allow for creative responses)
3. Does the speaker seem upset about losing his hands (eyes, legs, and mouth)? Why or why not?
   [No because he thinks about what he won't have to do anymore.]
4. Who or what is the speaker talking to in the last two lines?
   [He says it's the faithful light.] (again, encourage creative responses)

You may also want to point out that the speaker uses a double negative in the *if* clauses: Rather than saying, "anymore," he says, "no more." Discuss why the students think the speaker has chosen this form. Students may feel that the double negative is more informal and more emphatic than the grammatically correct form.

Option Two

> **Journal and/or poem; W; i**
> **20+ minutes/Homework**

If you are unable to find a copy of "Moonshadow," simply ask the students to write a short poem using the prompts found in the practice stage of the lesson. Encourage the students to write additional lines or to start fresh with their own set of *if I ever* situations.

The students could also write a paragraph about how their lives would change if they were to actually lose their sight, hearing, etc. How might they deal with the situation? Do they know of other people who have dealt with such an unexpected change in their lives? Have the students use the form "If I ever . . ." as in the writing prompt.

Option Three

> **Biography (Past tense); L, S, R, W; i & iiiii**
> **25+ minutes/ Homework**

Whether or not the students have been able to listen to the song "Moonshadow," this lesson provides students with the opportunity to think about what life must be like for people who are physically impaired, that is, physically challenged. How are such people treated in the society with which the students are familiar? What words are used to describe these people? Are some of these terms more positive than others? Does the society make an effort to include such people, or are they excluded from public life? You can explain that in the United States public buildings are made so that people in wheelchairs can have access to them and public transportation generally has lifts so that people who need them can still use the transportation. Also, events such as the Special Olympics give physically challenged people the opportunity to compete athletically, and a dance troupe made up of people in wheelchairs has performed on Broadway. Although much progress has been made to include rather than exclude physically challenged people, it can still be difficult for them to overcome their situations.

However, many people have overcome physical handicaps. Give the students the opportunity to discuss people they know of, famous or not, who have faced the challenges of physical impairment successfully. As an example, you can discuss Helen Keller (1880–1968), a famous American who, deaf, blind, and severely speech impaired as a result of an illness at the age of nineteen months, nevertheless was successfully graduated from Radcliffe College and became famous through the publication of her diary *The Story of My Life* (1902).

Two excerpts from Helen Keller's diary can be found in Appendix 3.10, Option Three, Part One (p. 111), and 3.10, Option Three, Part Two (p. 114). Please note that the second excerpt should not be read unless the students have already read the first passage. Each excerpt is followed by a work sheet with questions that you can use to facilitate a class discussion. To save class time, you may want to assign the reading(s) and questions as homework to be discussed the following day. If you have done lesson 1.11, you could link it to your discussion of the second excerpt from Helen Keller's diary.

To extend this lesson into a writing activity, you could ask your students to write a paragraph about someone who has overcome a physical handicap. If they are not familiar with such an example from their own lives, you may need to give the students some time to find information in the library. Or, if the students do not have access to such information, have them write about how the society they live in treats the physically challenged and what the students think about such treatment. Encourage the students to include a sentence or two in which they write about how they would actually deal with a similar experience.

Of course, you may have students who are themselves physically challenged. Before completing this lesson, you may want to ask them in private how they feel about having such a discussion in class. If they would prefer not to do so, then I would suggest respecting their wishes. If you think a student might feel awkward being asked such a queston, then I would suggest that you use your best judgment when determining whether or not to use this lesson.

3.11. Expressing Future Time: Speech

3.11a. Presentation

> **Word association; W; iii+ & iiiii**
> **Materials included**
> **10–20 minutes**

Write the name *Martin Luther King* on the board vertically. Ask the students to think of any nouns, adjectives, verbs, and adverbs that they associate with Martin Luther King, Jr. As the students make suggestions, you can write the individual words up on the board using the name as a guideline for the placing of each word. For example:

Minister
Assassinated
d**R**eam
Teacher
C**I**vil Rights Movement
African America**N**

Give the students time to think of word associations in groups of three or more and then discuss them as a class. You can refer to Appendix 3.11a for a completed version of this activity. If your students are not familiar with Martin Luther King, Jr., or the Civil Rights Movement in America, you can simply use the terms associated with his name in this activity as a means of introducing the students to Dr. King. If you choose this option, give the students time to familiarize themselves with any new vocabulary terms before discussing King's life. If you would like to give your students more information about King's life, refer to the time line in Appendix 2.2. Toward the end of the discussion about King, explain that on August 28, 1963, King led a peace march on Washington, DC, and gave a speech in front of the Lincoln Memorial to over 200,000 people in which he described his dream for America. With your students, discuss the symbolic significance of King's decision to give his speech in front of the Lincoln Memorial. The name of his speech is "I Have a Dream."

3.11b. Practice

> Cloze; L, S; i & iiiii
> 10–15 minutes

For this stage of the lesson, you will need to obtain a copy of Martin Luther King, Jr.'s speech "I Have a Dream" (1963). Often, you can find this speech in American history textbooks; if possible, you could also try the Internet. However, please note that King's works are copyrighted. Have the students complete a section of King's speech written as a cloze exercise. Omit the future tense verbs. A portion of the speech that works well with this lesson begins with the sentence "So I say to you my friends, that even though we must face the difficulties of today and tomorrow, I still have a dream." An example of a cloze passage based on just one sentence taken from the speech might look as follows.

I have a dream that my four little children (1) _____
_____ _____ _____ in a nation where
they (2) _____ _____ _____
_____ by the color of their skin but by the content of their
character.

1. will one day live
2. will not be judged

In this cloze example, I have included blanks for time expressions associated with the future tense and the passive future constructions. If you do the same, point this out to the students before they complete the cloze passage. Also, ask the students to read through the cloze passage and to circle any new vocabulary words. As a class discuss these new words. Once the students are comfortable with the vocabulary found in the text, tell them that you will read through the text and ask them to fill in the blanks as they listen to you read the speech.

To avoid the necessity of copyright permission, you could simply read through a portion of the speech and ask the students to note down the future tense verbs. However, be sure to preteach any new vocabulary terms before reading the passage.

Before the students complete the cloze passage, you could also use the word association technique to elicit words that appear in the section of the speech that you will introduce to your students. For example, to elicit the word *character* that appears in the cloze passage above, you could point to the *A* in *Martin* and say, "I'm thinking of a word that describes someone's personality. We say she or he has 'a lot of _____'" and so on until the term *character* has been elicited or introduced.

After the cloze passage has been completed, ask the students to consider why they think King has chosen to use the future tense repeatedly in his speech. The students should notice that King's use of the futures tense underscores the fact that racial equality did not exist at the time he gave his speech but that he hoped such equality would be achieved in the future. Once the students are familiar with King's speech, ask them to write a sentence in which they use their own words to summarize King's dream. Then they can discuss whether or not they think King's dream has been realized.

3.11c. Application

> Personalization; W; i & iiiii
> 15–20 minutes/Homework

After the students have discussed King's speech, ask them to imagine that they are going to give a speech in their own country. It will be given at a famous monument in the capital city in front of thousands of people. Ask the students to mimic King's style and to complete the sentence "I have a dream that one day. . . ." What is their dream for their country? This activity works best if students focus on one theme as King did, but, if they have more than one dream that they would like to share, encourage this as well. You can have the students give their "speeches" to the class. Be sure, however, that a context is set for each speech. Where is it being given? Who is speaking? Why is the speech important? You may want to give the students the opportunity to prepare their speeches at home before presenting them to the class. If you are teaching in a country in which the political situation is particularly sensitive, you may want to simply collect the students' speeches rather than requiring the students to share their work with their classmates. Use your discretion when deciding how far to take this activity.

If you have completed extended lesson 1.11 with your students, you can have them discuss how King demonstrated *agape* love in his life.

Appendix 3.1. Future Professions

Julie	**Jim**
• studies biology	• studies guitar
• applied to medical school	• has a great voice
• volunteers at a hospital	• collects rock 'n' roll music
• is interested in cancer research	• writes music

Sandra	**Dwayne**
• works part-time in a film developing lab	• likes to help people with their personal problems
• often goes to photo galleries	• studies psychology
• always wants camera equipment for gifts	• works part-time in a mental health clinic
• saves her money to buy film	• reads Freud and Jung, two psychologists

Gary	**Karen**
• studies geology	• knows many poems by heart
• knows the names and locations of all countries	• has a large collection of poetry books
• explores the desert	• often goes to poetry readings
• is fascinated by earthquake fault lines	• studies English poetry in school

Christine	**Pat**
• studies art	• admires Presidents Lincoln and Kennedy
• takes many classes in oil painting	• reads political journals and magazines
• often goes to art museums	• watches political debates on television
• studied in Italy for a summer	• studies political science

Jean	**Don**
• plays sports after school	• subscribes to computer magazines
• always watches basketball games	• writes computer programs for fun
• great at shooting baskets in basketball	• admires Bill Gates
• is very tall	• plans to study computer science

Appendix 3.2. Chart

Name _____

Name of Person	Person's Future Profession
1.	
2.	
3.	
4.	
5.	
6.	
7.	
8.	
9.	
10.	
11.	
12.	
13.	
14.	
15.	

Appendix 3.3. Alternative Situations

1. You are about to graduate from high school. You have the choice to go on to college or not.
   A. What will happen if you don't go to college?
   B. What will happen if you do go to college?

2. You are walking along a country road. The road comes to a fork, or divide, with one path going to the left and one path going to the right.
   A. What will happen if you go to the left?
   B. What will happen if you go to the right?

3. You are a heavy smoker.
   A. What will happen if you stop smoking?
   B. What will happen if you don't stop smoking?

4. You are nineteen and are thinking about getting married to your high school sweetheart.
   A. What will happen if you marry him or her?
   B. What will happen if you don't marry him or her?

5. You don't have a car, and you are thinking about buying one.
   A. What will happen if you buy a car?
   B. What will happen if you don't buy a car?

6. You have a chance to get a job with a different company.
   A. What will happen if you take the job?
   B. What will happen if you don't take the job?

7. You have the chance to move to another country for a year.
   A. What will happen if you decide to move?
   B. What will happen if you decide not to move?

Appendix 3.4. Inventions and Technological Developments

The radio

Television

Electricity

Cars

Refrigeration

Airplanes

Antibiotics

Atomic energy

The camera

The phonograph/record player

Trains

Appendix 3.7. Letter   Name(s) _____

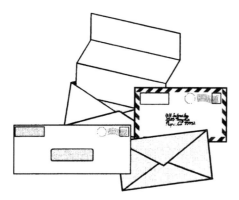

Paragraph 1: Introduce yourself to your reader and explain why you are concerned about the problem you've chosen to write about.

Paragraph 2: Explain what the situation was like in the past before the problem existed. Tell what caused the problem.

Paragraph 3: Explain what will happen if action is not taken to solve the problem. For example, "If we do not recycle paper and plant trees, the forests will soon disappear." Use *if* clauses to describe what will happen if certain things are done "If we recycle paper goods, then we will save the forests."

Appendix 3.8b. Poem   Name(s)_____

Put the following four stanzas into the correct order.

Robert Frost (1874–1963)

THE ROAD NOT TAKEN

STANZA a

Then took the other, as **just as fair,**
And having perhaps **the better claim,**
Because it was grassy and wanted wear;
Though as for that the passing there
Had worn them really about the same,

STANZA b

Two roads diverged in a yellow wood,
And sorry I could not travel both
And be one traveler, long I stood
And looked down one as far as I could
To where it bent in the undergrowth;

STANZA c

I shall be telling this with a sigh
Somewhere **ages and ages hence:**
Two roads diverged in a wood, and I—
I took the one less traveled by,
And that has made all the difference.

STANZA d

And both that morning equally lay
In leaves no step had trodden black.
Oh, I kept the first for another day!
Yet knowing how way leads on to way,
I doubted if I should ever come back.

Correct order: _____

---

just as fair: just as nice
the better claim: the better reason to take it
ages and ages hence: far in the future

Appendix 3.9b, Option One. Questions

Name(s)_____

The following *yes/no* questions are taken from the poem "Uphill" by Christina Rossetti. Using your imagination, answer the questions that the speaker of the poem asks about a journey she or he is taking to another town on foot. Since the questions are taken from a nineteenth-century poem, some of the expressions and their word order are not so common today. When this is the case, you will find a more modern equivalent of the word or question order in parentheses. The first one is done for you.

Christina Rossetti (1830–94)

UPHILL

1. Does the road wind (go) uphill all the way?

    No, sometimes the road goes downhill.

2. Will the day's journey take the whole long day?
    (Will the journey take all day?)

    _____

3. But is there for the night a resting place?
    (Is there a place to rest at night?)

    _____

4. May not the darkness hide it from my face?
    (Will the darkness hide the town from my sight?)

    _____

5. Shall I meet other wayfarers at night?
    (Will I meet other travelers on the road at night?)

    _____

6. Then must I knock, or call when just in sight?
    (Then must I knock on the door, or should I call out when I can see the inn?)

    _____

7. Shall I find comfort, travel-sore and weak?
    (Will I find a place to rest my sore and tired body?)

    _____

8. Will there be beds for me and all who seek?
    (Will there be enough beds for those who need them?)

    _____

Appendix 3.9b, Option Two. Questions

Name(s) _____

The following answers to *yes/no* questions are taken from the poem "Uphill" by Christina Rossetti. Using your imagination, write questions that you think are logical based on the answers already given. Since the answers are taken from a nineteenth-century poem, some of the expressions and their word order are not so common today. When this is the case, you will find a more modern equivalent of the word order in parentheses. The first one is done for you.

Christina Rossetti (1830–94)

UPHILL

1. Does the road go uphill all the way?
   Yes, to the very end.

2. _____
   From morn to night, my friend.
   (From morning until night, my friend.)

3. _____
   A roof for when the slow dark hours begin.
   (There's a place to stay when night begins.)

4. _____
   You cannot miss that inn.

5. _____
   Those who have gone before.

6. _____
   They will not keep you standing at that door.
   (They won't make you wait for service.)

7. _____
   Of labor you shall find the sum.
   (You will find work and wages.)

8. _____
   Yea, beds for all who come.
   (Yes, there's a place for everyone to sleep.)

Appendix 3.9c. Poem

Christina Rossetti (1830–94)

Uphill

Does the road wind uphill all the way?
    Yes, to the very end.
Will the day's journey take the whole long day?
    From morn to night,.my friend.

But is there for the night a resting place?
    A roof for when the slow dark hours begin.
May not the darkness hide **it** from my face?
    You cannot miss that inn.

Shall I meet other wayfarers at night?
    Those who have gone before.
Then must I knock, or call when **just in sight?**
    They will not keep you standing at that door.

Shall I find comfort, travel-sore and weak?
    Of labor you shall find the sum.
Will there be beds for me and all who seek?
    Yea, beds for all who come.

This poem is in the public domain.

---

it: *it* refers to the inn
just in sight: when the speaker can see the inn

Appendix 3.10c, Option Three. Part One

From *The Story of My Life* by Helen Keller (1902)

Adapted version: Passage 1

The following reading is adapted from the diary of Helen Keller, who lost her hearing, speech, and sight at the age of nineteen months because of an illness. When Helen Keller was six years old, Anne Sullivan, who was trained in teaching the blind, came to Helen Keller's home to try to educate her. In this passage, Helen Keller describes the moment when she first understood the meaning of the sign language used by the deaf.

The morning after my teacher came she led me into her room and gave me a doll. After I played with it a little while, Miss Sullivan slowly spelled into my hand the word "d-o-l-l." I was at once interested in this finger game and tried **to imitate** her movements. When I finally succeeded in making the letters correctly, I was full of childish pleasure and pride. Running downstairs to my mother, I held up my hand and made the letters for *doll*. I did not know that I was spelling a word or even that words existed; I was simply making my fingers go in **monkeylike imitation**. In the days that followed, I learned to spell in this way a great many words, among them *pin, hat, cup*, and a few verbs like *sit, stand*, and *walk*, but I didn't understand what the words meant.

Miss Sullivan tried to teach me the difference between c-u-p and w-a-t-e-r, but I kept confusing the two words, and I couldn't understand what they meant. I became frustrated with her attempts to teach me, and, picking up the doll, I threw it on the floor, breaking its porcelain head. I felt neither sorrow nor regret. I had not loved the doll. In the still, dark world in which I lived there were no strong emotions or tenderness. I felt my teacher sweep up the pieces from the doll. Then she brought me my hat, and I knew that I was going into the warm sunshine. This thought, if a **wordless** feeling can be called a thought, made me jump up and down with pleasure.

We walked down the path to **a well-house,** attracted by the smell of flowers growing on its little roof. Someone was drawing water and my teacher placed my hand under the spout. As the cool stream of water ran over my hand, on the other she spelled the word water, first slowly, then rapidly. I stood still. All my attention was focused on the motion of her fingers. Suddenly, I felt I understood the mystery of language. I knew then that "w-a-t-e-r" meant the wonderful cool something that was flowing over my hand. That living word awakened my soul, gave it light, hope, joy, set it free!

---

to imitate: to copy the movement of her fingers
monkeylike imitation: to copy a motion like a monkey does without understanding what it means
wordless: Helen Keller had no words to describe her feelings or thoughts.
a well-house: a well that has a small roof to protect it

I left the well-house eager to learn. Everything had a name, and each name gave birth to a new thought. . . . I learned a great many words that day. I do not remember what they all were; but I do know that *mother, father, sister, teacher* were among them. . . . I had now the key to all language, and I was eager to learn and to use it.

The excerpt is adapted from *The Story of My Life* which is in the public domain. Questions © 1999 University of Michigan.

Questions for Part One   Name(s)_____

1. When Anne Sullivan spelled the word *doll* into Helen's hand, what did she want Helen to understand?

2. Why does Helen say she "felt" her teacher sweep up the pieces of the doll?

3. Since Helen had no words or images to express her thoughts, what kind of thoughts do you think she had? How did she think?

4. In the last paragraph, Helen says, "I had now the key to all language." In your own words, describe what she meant by the "key to language."

5. Helen Keller learned English, French, German, and Latin using sign language. What do you think about these accomplishments? How might you feel in her place?

Appendix 3.10c, Option Three. Part Two

From *The Story of My Life* by Helen Keller (1902)

Adapted version: Passage 2

In this next adapted excerpt from Helen Keller's diary, she describes how she came to understand the meaning of abstract words such as *think* and *love,* words that represent feelings and thoughts that cannot be touched.

I remember the morning that I first asked the meaning of the word, "love." This was before I knew many words. I had found some **violets** in the garden and brought them to my teacher. Miss Sullivan put her arm gently around me and spelled into my hand, "I love Helen."

"What is love?" I asked.

She brought me near to her and said, "It is here," pointing to my heart. Her words **puzzled** me very much because I did not then understand anything unless I touched it.

I smelled the violets in her hand and asked, half in words, half in signs, a question which meant, "Is love the sweet smell of flowers?"

"No," said my teacher.

As I thought about her answer, I felt the warm sun shining on us.

"Is the sun love?" I asked, pointing in the direction from which the warmth came.

It seemed to me that there was nothing more beautiful than the warmth of the sun which made all things grow. But Miss Sullivan shook her head, and I was greatly puzzled and disappointed. I thought it was strange that my teacher could not show me love.

A day or two later, I was **putting beads of different sizes onto a string**—two large beads, three small ones, and so on to make a necklace. I had made many mistakes. Then I noticed an error in the order of the beads, and for a moment I stopped to think about how I should have ordered the beads. Miss Sullivan touched my forehead and spelled, "Think."

Suddenly, I understood that the word *think* was the name of the process that was going on in my head. This was my first understanding of an abstract idea.

For a long time, I did not move—I was thinking of the meaning for the word "love." I asked my teacher if love was the sunshine after the rain.

---

violets: small, purple flowers
to be puzzled: to be confused; to not understand something
putting beads of different sizes onto a string: Helen was making a necklace by herself. She used small, round colored beads.

In simpler words than these, which at that time I could not have understood, she explained, "Love is something like the rain clouds. You can not touch the clouds, but you feel the rain and know the clouds are there, and the rain makes everything grow. You cannot touch love either; but you can feel the sweetness it gives to life. Without love you would not be happy or want to play."

Then I understood the meaning of love. It was a beautiful truth—I felt that there were **invisible** lines reaching between my spirit and the spirits of others.

The excerpt is adapted from *The Story of My Life* which is in the public domain. Questions © 1999 University of Michigan Press.

---

invisible: something that cannot be seen with the eyes

Questions for Part Two   Name(s)_____

1. Why couldn't Helen understand the meaning of the word *love?*

2. Why did Helen think that violets and the warmth of the sun might be love? Her teacher told her these things were not love. Do you agree?

3. How are the words *think* and *love* different from words like *doll* and *water?*

4. In your own words, explain how Helen finally understood the meaning of the word *think.*

5. How would you define *love* for someone who did not know what the word *love* meant?

6. When Helen finally understood the meaning of love, how did she feel? How would you feel in her place?

Appendix 3.11a. Word Associations

Minister

Assassinated

d**R**eam

Teacher

CIvil Rights Movement

Africa**N** American

Love

Understanding

pro**T**ests

speec**H**es

d**E**monstrations

p**R**eacher

King

s**I**t-ins

Nonviolence

dese**G**regation

Chapter 4
The Present Perfect

Itemized Reference List

Skill Areas		Group Work	
Listening	L	Individual	i
Speaking	S	Pair	ii
Reading	R	Small Group	iii+
Writing	W	Class	iiiii

Structure		Activity	Skills	Groups	Appendix
Supplementary Activities					
4.1.	The Present Perfect	Question formation	L, S, W	i & ii & iiiii	
4.2.	The Present Perfect + *Already/Yet*	Personalization	L, S	i & ii & iiiii	
4.3.	*Have You Ever . . . ?*	Visual focus	L, S	iii+ & iiiii	
4.4.	Present Perfect + Time Words	Visual focus	L, S	iii+ & iiiii	
4.5.	The Use of the Present Perfect	Research	R, W	i & ii & iii+ & iiiii	133
Extended Lessons					
4.6.	The Present Perfect: Autobiography				
4.6a.	Presentation	Rule matching	R	i & ii	
4.6b.	Practice	Question formation	L, S	ii & iiiii	
4.6c.	Application	Information gap	L, S, R, W	i & ii	
4.6d.	Review	Error correction	R, W	i & ii & iiiii	134
4.6e.	Practice	Information gap	L, S	iii+ & iiiii	
4.7.	Tag Questions + Present Perfect: Job Interview				
4.7a.	Presentation	Dialogue	L, S	i & ii & iiiii	135
4.7b.	Practice	Intonation	L, S	ii & iiiii	
4.7c.	Application	Dialogue	L, S, R, W	ii & iii+ & iiiii	136
4.8.	The Use of the Present Perfect: Poem				
4.8a.	Presentation	Poem	L, S, R	ii & iiiii	138
4.8b.	Practice	Changing tenses	L, S, R	ii & iiiii	
4.8c.	Application	Second identity	W	i	

Supplementary Activities

4.1. The Present Perfect

> Question formation; L, S, W; i & ii & iiiii

On the board, write the name of a well-known person who is still living and his or her occupation and accomplishments, as has been done below for Alice Walker, an African American writer.

Alice Walker—African American (b. 1944)
- Writer
- Two short story collections
- Four novels: *The Color Purple* (1985) won a Pulitzer Prize, and the director Steven Spielberg made a movie based on the novel.

Then have your students ask questions about this person using the present perfect and the present perfect progressive based on the information written on the board. For example, in the case of Alice Walker, students might ask:

- Has she written any short stories?
- How many novels has she written?
- What has she written?
- Have any of her books been made into movies?
- Have you read any of her novels?
- What has she been doing?

After the students have successfully practiced the use of the present perfect and present perfect progressive, encourage them to form questions using the simple past. In this case, the students could ask:

Who made *The Color Purple* into a movie?
What novels did Alice Walker write?
When did Alice Walker win the Pulitzer Prize?

In pairs, have the students practice asking and answering such questions. You may need to make a few more examples for the students to discuss. Once the students are comfortable with the format of the activity, have them write similar information about an artist, a writer, a scientist, etc., from their own or another country. Ideally, you should have the students ask questions about the lives of people they have previously discussed in class so that the vocabulary used in the activity will not distract them as they practice the present perfect form. Then have the students write up the information on the board. As a class, have the students ask and answer the related questions about a person. You may want to give students the opportunity to do some research at home about the person they've chosen to work on so that they will be better prepared to answer questions in class. This exercise can also spark an interesting discussion about the pronunciation of names in other countries and the accomplishments of people in a student's country of origin.

4.2. The Present Perfect + *Already/Yet*

> **Personalization; L, S; i & ii & iiiii**

List seven things on the board that you usually do during the week. Try to select activities that serve to express your personality and interests. Discuss these activities in the present tense with the students, making sure that they understand any new vocabulary items. Then, explain to the students that you have done some of these things already but you haven't done all of them yet. Have the students ask you, "Have you already . . . ?" Answer using *have* or *haven't* with a general explanation. For example, "No I haven't gone shopping yet because I usually go shopping on Friday afternoons." After you've gone through the list with the students, have each of them make his or her own list of weekly activities using the simple present. Make sure the students focus on activities that they feel are unique to them; otherwise, you'll end up with unoriginal responses such as "I have already eaten breakfast today." Students can then ask one another questions about their lists using the present perfect with *already* or *yet* as appropriate. You can use this as a warm-up activity by having the students keep their lists and pair up with someone different on the following day.

4.3. *Have You Ever . . . ?*

> **Visual focus; L, S; iii+ & iiiii**
> **Materials included**

Bring in a few pictures that present an intriguing situation—covers from the *New Yorker* or pictures from a calendar—and discuss what's going on in the pictures with the students. Have them try to imagine where the scene is, who the people are, what time of year it is, etc. The idea is to give the students the opportunity to familiarize themselves with the content of the pictures before using it to practice asking, "Have you ever . . . ?" For example, consider the illustration of a birthday party found in Appendix 1.4. Once the students have had the chance to discuss new vocabulary items related to the picture, they could ask one another questions such as

Have you ever gone to a birthday party?
Have you ever baked a birthday cake?
Have you ever planned a birthday party for someone?
Have you ever blown out candles on a cake?
Have you ever made a birthday wish?

You may want to look for pictures that reflect the cultural traditions of your students. If you bring in enough pictures to divide your class into groups of three or four, you can have each group come up with a description and a set of *have you ever* questions for their picture. Then, in turn, each group can present their picture to the class and ask their classmates a series of *have you ever* questions. Encourage the students to ask follow-up questions: if someone says that he or she has been to a birthday party, the students should ask for details about the experience. You can point out that when additional details are given about an experience, people usually change to the past tense: "Yes, I've been to a birthday party. I went to my friend's sixteenth birthday. It was a great party," etc.

4.4. Present Perfect + Time Words

> **Visual focus; L, S; iii+ & iiiii**
> **Materials included**

If you have completed activity 4.3, then use the same pictures as the basis for this activity. If you choose to use new illustrations, then be sure to give the students the chance to familiarize themselves with the vocabulary needed to describe the situations depicted in each picture. Also, since this activity is meant to reinforce the students' understanding of verb tenses, it should only be used after the students have already had some practice using the past and present tenses, the future tense, the present perfect and present perfect progressive, *and* the time expressions associated with these tenses.

To model this activity, have the students focus on a picture that they have previously discussed and ask the students to answer the following questions in turn.

1. What has already happened?
2. What is still happening?
3. What have the people been doing?
4. What hasn't happened yet?
5. What will happen next?

Encourage the students to respond imaginatively to the questions and to come up with more than one possible response. For example, in answer to the question, "What has already happened?" students referring to the illustration of a birthday party found in Appendix 1.4 could say:

> Someone has already baked a cake and planned the party. People have already arrived. They have already started to sing "Happy Birthday." The birthday girl who is blowing out the candles has already made a wish.

This activity helps to check the students' comprehension of the differences in meaning suggested by the time expressions and/or verb tenses used in each question. Again, it is important to be sure that students are able to verbalize the content of a given picture in the present tense before they apply the past, future, present perfect, and present perfect progressive tenses to a discussion of the picture's content; otherwise, they may be confused by new vocabulary items before they even begin to analyze the verb tenses involved in answering the questions.

Write the questions on the board and have small groups of students describe their group's picture and then ask one another the questions written on the board. You can then have each group present its picture and ask their classmates the five time sequence questions.

If you'd like, add other questions to the sequence such as, What has just happened? or What happened a short time ago?

4.5. The Use of the Present Perfect

> **Research; R, W; i & ii & iii+ & iiiii**
> **Materials included**

For homework, ask the students to select a short magazine and/or newspaper article and have them underline the present perfect forms found in the text. Point out to the students that they may have to look at a few articles to find examples of the present perfect. The students should write down bibliographic information such as the name of the magazine, the title of the article, the author, the date, and the page. Ask them to copy out the sentences with the present perfect. Then ask them to write out their responses to the following questions.

1. Is the present perfect used very often?
2. What explanations can you give for the use of the present perfect in the sentences you have found?

You may want to model this activity for the students by bringing in an article you have found and analyzing the results as a class before the students work independently. To help the students organize their work, have them use the work sheet found in Appendix 4.5.

You can also have them bring in their articles and a brief summary to share in small groups. Then the students can discuss their findings in pairs or groups and then as a class.

Extended Lessons

4.6. The Present Perfect: Autobiography

4.6a. Presentation

> **Rule matching; R; i & ii**
> **15 minutes**

This lesson focuses on a few of the rules that are generally taught with the use of the present perfect. I have chosen to use rules based on those given by Betty Azar in her book *Fundamentals of English Grammar (1992),* but you may choose to reword the rules or to use rules that are stated differently. The rules indicate that the present perfect is used in the following situations.

A. Unspecified time in the past and using *already, yet, recently,* etc.	B. A repeated action in the past	C. Length of time using *for* or *since*

To demonstrate these rules in use, write a short overview of your life that explains some of the more interesting things that you have or haven't done in your life from childhood until the present. (If you prefer, write about someone else.) Take care to use sentences that exhibit the three rules that you want to present. You can give the students reading practice by having pairs of students take turns reading aloud sentences from the passage. You may want to preteach new vocabulary words. While the students are reading in pairs, write the rules up on the board as has previously been shown.

Have the students copy the board and take a moment to discuss any questions the students might have about the rules. Then ask them to reread your paragraph silently, writing each present perfect verb and a bit of additional information in the appropriate column. For example, for the sentence "I have traveled in Europe," the students should write, *has traveled in Europe* in column A since it is an action that took place at an unspecified time in the past.

4.6b. Practice

> **Question formation; L, S; ii & iiiii**
> **15 minutes**

Once the students have had time to read through the overview of your life, put them in pairs and have them compare their results. This is a good time to go around to the various groups and clarify the application of each rule, particularly the difference between rules A and B. Then, as a class, take time to consider how the students would form questions to ask for the information related to a verb in a given column. For example:

A	B	C
Why has she . . . ?	How often has she . . . ?	How long . . . ?
What has she . . . ?	How many times . . . ?	
Where has she . . . ?		
What hasn't she done yet?		

Give the students the opportunity to ask you their questions. When you answer their questions, you can encourage the students to ask you for more information about your response. Point out that when people give more information about an experience, they usually change to the simple past: "I've traveled in Europe. I went there in 1990 and stayed for five years, so I traveled around in Western and Eastern Europe."

4.6c. Application

> **Information gap; L, S, R, W; i & ii**
> **15 minutes/Homework**

Once the students have worked through the text about your life, ask them to write about themselves as a homework assignment. Have them write a paragraph of at least ten sentences. Make it clear that the students should write information that is uniquely about them and that they should try to write sentences that exemplify the rules that have been presented. After twenty minutes or on the next day, put the students in pairs. Have them make three columns again on a piece of paper and put the rules at the heads of the columns. Then, as one student listens to his or her partner read, he or she should note down the present perfect form of a given verb in the correct column. After the students have read their brief autobiographies, have them ask one another questions about each other's lives using their notes to help them form questions in the present perfect. Some students may not feel comfortable writing about themselves; if so, let them choose someone else to write about. You may want to collect the students' writings and correct the grammar mistakes related to the use of the present perfect before they share their writings in pairs.

4.6d. Review

> **Error correction; R, W; i & ii & iiiii**
> **Materials included**
> **10–20 minutes**

Collect the students' writings. Read through them, noting any sentences that contain grammatical errors related to the use of the present perfect. Type up these sentences to make an error correction work sheet. Try to group related errors together. Also, when typing up the handout, correct any errors that are not directly related to the present perfect form. (See Appendix 4.6d for a sample error correction work sheet; the sentences on this work sheet were written by intermediate-level ESL students.) Have the students work individually to find and correct the errors. Then have them work in pairs to compare their results. As a class, you may then correct the work sheet all at once, or you may choose to review sections of the work sheet as a warm-up or review activity in subsequent lessons. The overhead projector is particularly useful for checking such an exercise.

4.6e. Practice

> **Information gap; L, S; iii+ & iiiii**
> **20 minutes**

Using information that you collect from the students' writings, create a "Find Someone Who" handout that pertains to your students' experiences and has the present perfect form and just enough information to make the context clear. For example:

> Find someone who has . . .
> eaten a snake   _____
> traveled in Cambodia   _____
> climbed a volcano   _____

As a warm-up activity, preteach any vocabulary from the list that may be new to the students. Model asking a question using the present perfect form with the new vocabulary: "Have you eaten a snake?" Also, model how to answer *yes/no* questions with "Yes, I have" or "No, I haven't" as may be presented in the students' textbook.

Once this presentation has been done, ask the students to stand up and circulate asking asking questions to complete their "Find Someone Who" list. Make sure the students ask questions using the present perfect. Also, they should ask only one person one question and then ask someone else a question. This keeps the activity moving at a faster pace.

After the students have had about ten minutes to gather information, you may want to point out to students that native speakers rarely answer such questions with a simple "Yes, I have" or "No, I haven't." Ask a student to ask you the first question, in this case, "Have you eaten a snake?" Then answer using different responses. For example:

> No, but my brother has.
> No, I'm a vegetarian and don't eat any kind of meat.
> No, I considered the idea once but changed my mind.
> No, but I've eaten bear meat before.

In small groups, have them practice answering the questions in a more natural way than simply saying, "Yes, I have" or "No, I haven't." If you don't have time to make a list based on your students' experiences, simply make a list with general information such as "Find someone who has visited Canada." However, using information based on the lives of your students gives them the opportunity to get to know one another better and makes the activity more relevant to the students.

As a class, have the students share who has done what. Encourage those who have done something on the list to share more information about their experiences. Again, you can point out that when people give more details about an experience, they usually change to the simple past as in the following example.

Student A: Yes, I've climbed a volcano.
Student B: What was it like?
Student A: Well, it wasn't an active volcano. It was Mt. Shasta in Northern California, and it was very cold at the top.

Encourage the students to keep the conversation going by asking their partner relevant questions.

4.7. Tag Questions + Present Perfect: Job Interview

4.7a. Presentation

> Dialogue; L, S; i & ii & iiiii
> Materials included
> 15 minutes

To introduce the use of tag questions with the present perfect try the following extended lesson, which is based on a job interview. This particular lesson is based on jobs found in a high-tech industry. If your students plan to look for jobs in other fields, you may want to adapt the materials found in this lesson to the interests of your students. Also, if your students are not familiar with the job interview process, you may need to take the time to explain this process to them.

On the board, draw the profiles of two individuals, in this case, Diane and Henry, who are facing each other, about two feet apart.

Diane   Henry

Tell the students that they'll be hearing a conversation between a woman named Diane and a man named Henry, but don't tell them what the conversation is about. If you can't prerecord this conversation, you can indicate who is speaking by simply pointing to the appropriate profile for either speaker in turn. The first time the students hear the dialogue, they should try to determine what the situation is.

Diane: You haven't been in the country long, have you?
Henry: No, I've only been here for two months now.
Diane: And you've been looking for a job in computers, haven't you?
Henry: That's right, I have a degree in computer science.
Diane: So, you're applying for a position as a computer programmer in our company.
Henry: I think that I would do well in this position.
Diane: Let's see, you've worked for Toshiba, haven't you?
Henry: Yes, as a matter of fact, I worked in Japan for three years.
Diane: So you're fluent in Japanese, right?
Henry: Well, my Japanese is pretty good.
Diane: You know our company will be doing business with Japan, don't you?
Henry: That's one reason I'm here today.
Diane: You haven't thought about moving back to Japan, have you?
Henry: I'm open to the idea.
Diane: Well, if you take this job, that would be a possibility.

Discuss what the situation is with the students and the role each of the speakers plays. To check the students' comprehension, have them listen to the dialogue again but this time ask them to note down the verbs that Diane uses in her questions. Then, together with the students, create a list of verbs on the board. In pairs, have the students refer to the verbs to recreate the questions that Diane asks Henry and then discuss the sequence of questions as a class. Once you're sure that the students comprehend the dialogue, give them a copy of Appendix 4.7a or simply make an overhead copy of the handout. On this handout, the dialogue has been written out, but the tag questions have been left off. Ask the students to work together in pairs to fill in the blanks. Check the students' answers using the overhead. You may want to point out that the use of *right* is more colloquial than using the present perfect form. Then have students practice the dialogue in pairs, taking turns as first Diane and then Henry.

4.7b. Practice

> Intonation; L, S; ii & iiiii
> 10 minutes

This interview provides a good opportunity to introduce how intonation affects the meaning of a question. Read through the dialogue and have the students mark if the pitch of the tag goes up or down and what the significance of the intonation might be. Ask the students to guess what Diane already knows or doesn't know about Henry based on the pitch you have given each tag. Have the students practice the dialogue emphasizing their intonation.

Examples
   Diane: You haven't been in the country long, have you?
   (Diane already knows this information.)

   Diane: You haven't thought about moving back to Japan, have you?
   (Diane doesn't know if Henry has thought about moving back to Japan.)

4.7c. Application

> Dialogue; L, S, R, W; ii & iii+ & iiiii
> Materials included
> 25 minutes/Homework

With the class, generate a list of important categories for a job history or résumé: professional information, education, hobbies. Then give pairs of students one of the three job histories from Appendix 4.7c.

Ask each pair of students to write a dialogue between the interviewer from the import/export company ARG and the applicant whose job history they've been given. Encourage the students to use tag questions when they create their dialogues and remind them that the interviewer only knows the information found in the job history. Suggest that the students ask questions to get information that is not in the job history. The interviewees can then respond imaginatively to these questions. You may want to give the students time to work on the dialogue together outside of class.

Give the students who have worked on the same job history the opportunity to share their dialogues and choose the one they like best. Then have the representatives from each group perform their dialogue for the class. The class can then decide which of the three candidates should get the job.

4.8. The Use of the Present Perfect: Poem

4.8a. Presentation

> **Poem; L, S, R; ii & iiiii**
> **Materials included**
> **10 minutes**

For a change of pace, consider using the poem "This Is Just to Say" by William Carlos Williams (1883–1963), an American poet, as a way to illustrate the tone and meaning of the present perfect.

For "This Is Just to Say," you may want to preteach the words *plums, icebox,* and *forgive.* You may also need to explain that people in the United States often eat fruit for breakfast and sometimes put it on toast or cereal. Discuss the idea of leaving a note for someone and the possibility of putting it on the refrigerator using a magnet. You can elicit these ideas and vocabulary by asking such questions as

1. What do people in the United States generally eat for breakfast? Do they eat fruit for breakfast? If so, what kinds of fruit? etc.
2. Where do people in the United States generally leave notes for one another?
3. What is an old-fashioned word for *refrigerator?*

Project the poem on an overhead using the enlarged copy found in Appendix 4.8a or just write the poem on the board. You could also simply dictate the poem to the students. Then have the students read the poem silently to themselves.

Read the poem to the students. After the reading, have the students work in pairs to answer the following questions.

1. What is the first line of the poem?
2. When do you think the note was written?
3. Who wrote the note and to whom did he or she write it?
4. How can you tell this note is an apology?
5. Has the note been read yet?

When responding to question number one, the students should notice that the title of the poem also serves as the poem's first line, making this poem a note to someone. When the students discuss their responses to question five, you can point out that the note has been read because they have read it! This makes for an interesting discussion about the poem's intended audience.

4.8b. Practice

> **Changing tenses; L, S, R; ii & iiiii**
> **5 minutes**

Ask the students why they think the poet chose to use the present tense in the first line rather than the simple past. Have them read the poem in pairs, changing the present perfect to the simple past.

> This is just to say
> I *ate*
> the plums
> that were in the icebox

As a class, discuss their ideas. Help the students to come to the following conclusions regarding Williams's use of the present perfect.

1. He uses the present perfect because he is writing a note about a finished action that affects the person who will later read the note.
2. He uses the present perfect to announce something he has done and then changes to the simple past to give more details about what happened.
3. He uses the present perfect simply because it "softens" the tone of his message. (Some students may think that the use of the present perfect sounds more formal than the use of the simple past. Others may have difficulty sensing a tonal difference between the two forms. In either case, the students' responses can lead to an intriguing class discussion.)

4.8c. Application

> **Second identity; W; i**
> **10–15 minutes/Homework**

Have the students imagine that they are the person the note was written to and ask them to write a letter back to the author of the original note. Remind them to use the present perfect tense at least once in their reply. Share the results as a class. You could have the students write their notes in prose form and then in a more poetic form that mimics Williams's style.

You could also give the students the option of writing a note of apology to someone they have wronged in the past. However, if you have your students write such a personal note, you may want to tell them that their letters will not be shared with other students in the class. Again, ask them to use the present perfect at least once in their letter.

This activity can easily be depersonalized by having the students take on a second identity that is based on a well-known person who has previously been discussed in class. For example, a student could assume the identity of Vincent van Gogh (discussed in activity 1.2) and write a letter of apology to Vincent's brother Theo for having borrowed so much money.

This extended lesson can readily be adapted to other poems in which the use of the present perfect dramatically affects the tone of the poem such as "I Have Been Acquainted with the Night" by Robert Frost (1874–1963) and the poem "The Negro Speaks of Rivers" by Langston Hughes (1902–67).

Appendix 4.5. Present Perfect

Name(s)_____

Name of newspaper or magazine: _____

Name of article: _____

Author (if stated): _____

Date of publication: _____ Page(s) _____

Summary of article

Sentences using the present perfect

1.   Is the present perfect used very often?

2.   What explanations can you give for the use of the present perfect in the sentences you have found? (Choose up to five sentences to analyze.)

Appendix 4.6d. Error Correction Work Sheet

Name(s)_____

The Present Perfect

1. I have taken a driver's license test since 1990.

2. I have drived a car to school since 1987.

3. Since 1989, I've swum in the pool.

4. I have gone skiing for ten years.

5. I have visited San Francisco on October 27.

6. I have been in a traffic accident in 1994.

7. I have talked with her at that time.

Appendix 4.7a. Dialogue Name(s)_____

Present Perfect Tags
with Diane and Henry

Diane: You haven't been in the country long, _____?

Henry: No, I've only been here for two months now.

Diane: And you've been looking for a job in computers, _____?

Henry: That's right, I have a degree in computer science.

Diane: So, you're applying for a position as a computer programmer in our company.

Henry: I think that I would do well in this position.

Diane: Let's see, you've worked for Toshiba, _____?

Henry: Yes, as a matter of fact, I worked in Japan for three years.

Diane: So you're fluent in Japanese, right?

Henry: Well, my Japanese is pretty good.

Diane: You know our company will be doing business with Japan, _____?

Henry: That's one reason I'm here today.

Diane: You haven't thought about moving back to Japan, _____?

Henry: I'm open to the idea.

Diane: Well, if you take this job, that could be a possibility.

Appendix 4.7c. Job History

The company ARG, which imports stereo equipment from Japan and South Korea, is looking for a new manager for the import office. She or he should have knowledge of the Asian market, international trade, finance, and Asian languages. She or he should also be computer literate.

The following people have applied for the managerial position with ARG. Who do you think would be the best candidate? Why?

A. Jennifer Lewis

Professional Experience
1. Has organized an international trade fair between Japan and the United States
2. Has worked for three years in an import/export company dealing with Japan
3. Has coordinated an office of twenty staff members

Education and Special Training
1. Has completed courses in computer programming
2. Has received a degree in finance from the University of Michigan
3. Has spent years studying Japanese

Personal Interests
1. Has traveled in Japan
2. Has been interested in Japanese art for many years

B. Tom Coleman

Professional Experience
1. Has worked for five years as a financial consultant for IBM in Utah
2. Has developed a budget plan for IBM in Utah
3. Has done consulting work for companies who work in import/export

Education and Special Training
1. Has earned a degree in computer science and an MBA
2. Has knowledge of computer programs
3. Has attended seminars on business consulting

Personal Interests
1. Has traveled widely in Europe
2. Has played tennis since high school

C. Daniel Kim

Professional Experience

1. Has worked in Japan as a business English teacher
2. Has worked for an American company as an accountant
3. Has prepared tax documents

Education and Special Training

1. Has received an MBA with an emphasis in international studies
2. Has had training in the use of computers
3. Has 2 years of college-level Japanese

Personal Interests

1. Has lived and worked in Japan
2. Has traveled in Korea
3. Has grown up speaking Korean and English

Appendix 4.8a. Poem

William Carlos Williams (1883–1963)

THIS IS JUST TO SAY

I have eaten
the plums
that were in
the icebox
and which
you were probably
saving for breakfast.

Forgive me
they were delicious
so sweet
and so cold.

Chapter 5

* virtually all modals can express both logical probability and social interaction

Modal Auxiliary Verbs

Itemized Reference List

Skill Areas		Group Work	
Listening	L	Individual	i
Speaking	S	Pair	ii
Reading	R	Small Group	iii+
Writing	W	Class	iiiii

Structure	Activity	Skills	Groups	Appendix
Supplementary Activities				
5.1. The Use of *Have to, Get to,* and *Need to*	Intonation	L, S	ii & iiiii	
5.2. The Use of *Must* and *Must Not*	Role play/Register	L, S	ii & iiiii	157
5.3. Modals of Possibility	Visual focus	L, S, W	i & iiiii	158
5.4. Modals of Advice	Visual focus/ Research	L, S, W	i & iiiii	160
5.5. Modals of Possibility and Advice	Personalization	L, S, W	i & iii+	
5.6. Modals of Advice and Possibility	Problem/Solution	R, W	i & ii & iii+ & iiiii	
5.7. Using Modals	Second identity/ Visual focus	L, S	ii & iiiii	
5.8. Using Modals	Cartoons	L, S, W	i & iii+	
5.9. Using *Should* to Express Indecision	Making choices	L, S	i & ii & iiiii	
Extended Lessons				
5.10. *Can* and *Could:* Personalization				
5.10a. Presentation	Question formation	L, S	ii & iiiii	
5.10b. Practice	Personalization	L, S	ii	
5.10c. Application	Summarizing	W	i	
5.10d. Review	Error correction	R, W	i & ii & iiiii	
5.11. Giving Advice: Advice Columnist				
5.11a. Presentation	Advice columnist	L, S	iiiii	
5.11b. Practice	Discourse analysis	L, S, R	i & ii & iiiii	162
5.11c. Application: Option One	Letter writing	W	i & ii	
5.11c. Application: Option Two	Letter writing	W	i & iii+ & iiiii	
5.12. Expressing Preferences: Song				
5.12a. Presentation and Practice	Preferences	L, S	ii & iiiii	
5.12b. Practice	Cloze exercise	L, S	i & ii & iiiii	
5.12c. Application: Option One	Drawing	L, S	i & iiiii	
5.12c. Application: Option Two	Songwriting	W	i & iiiii	

139

Supplementary Activities

5.1.   The Use of *Have to, Get to,* and *Need to*

> Intonation; L, S; ii & iiiii

When you're presenting the modal *have to,* it's a good time to introduce the contrasting form *get to,* which is often overlooked in grammar textbooks. To present this form, make two columns on the board. In one, list three things you have to do over the weekend; in the other, list three things you get to do over the weekend. Have the students guess why you wrote the two different columns of verbs on the board. Explain that you have to do the things on the left but that you get to do the things on the right. You can use your intonation to show that the auxiliary *get to* with a rising intonation implies a sense of pleasure on the part of the speaker while the use of *have to* with a dropping intonation suggests obligation on the part of the speaker. Here's a sample list of verbs.

This weekend I . . .

have to	get to
pay the bills	go for a long walk
go shopping	go out to dinner
wash the windows	take time to read a magazine

Once you've discussed the listed verbs and addressed any vocabulary questions, have the students take turns asking you, "What do you have to do this weekend?" and "What do you get to do this weekend?" Then have the students make their own columns and ask one another the same questions in pairs. This activity can be used as a warm-up or for review on following days by having students pair up with a new partner. Encourage the students to use rising and falling intonation when responding to a question. (Generally, a neutral tone is used to ask a question with either *have to* or *get to.*) You can also point out that *need to* can be used as an auxiliary to express something that is necessary for the speaker to do but not necessarily obligatory. When using *need to,* the speaker may lower the intonation to express displeasure, or the intonation may remain flat, or neutral, to simply express the fact that something needs to be done.

5.2. The Use of *Must* and *Must Not*

> **Role play/Register; L, S; ii & iiiii**
> **Materials included**

It is important that students understand the social context in which *must* is used to express necessity or prohibition; otherwise, they may mistakenly use the modal in inappropriate situations. To help students understand that *must,* when it means *necessity* or *prohibition,* is generally used when someone in a position of responsibility or authority is speaking to a person in that individual's care or under his or her authority, you can model a short dialogue between a father and his sixteen-year-old son who wants to go to a party with his friends. Let the students guess what the situation is based on the short dialogue. For example:

Father: Well, you can go but you must be home by eleven o'clock.
Son: Can't I stay out later? All the guys will be at the party until midnight.
Father: Sorry, eleven o'clock is it.

Appendix 5.2 includes a number of situations requiring the use of *must* and *must not.* You may choose to create other scenarios that are more relevant to the background of your students.

Have pairs of students come up with a brief dialogue for their situations and then have each pair act out their dialogue for the class. Encourage the students to use *must* and/or *must not* in their role play. Ask the other students to guess the situation from the information provided in the dialogue. On the board, write the list of situations as they occur. Then ask the students what the situations share in common. Elicit the following responses.

- A person in a position of authority or responsibility is talking to someone under that person's authority or in his or her care.
- The use of *must* or *must not* sounds authoritative.

After you've discussed the use of *must* and *must not,* take a few minutes to have the students think of situations where it wouldn't be appropriate to use *must* or *must not* and would be better to use another modal. For example:

When talking to a guest at your house
When giving a friend advice
When talking to your peers
When talking to someone who is in a position of authority over you

5.3. Modals of Possibility: *Could, Might, May, Maybe, Will Probably,* and *Will*

> **Visual focus; L, S, W; i & iiiii**
> **Materials included**

To give students a way to visualize the degrees of possibility found in modals, share the modal thermometer in Appendix 5.3a with your students.

You can make the presentation of the modal thermometer more interactive by giving students a copy of the thermometer with the modals removed (a copy is provided in Appendix 5.3b). Then review the modals of possibility: *could, might, may, maybe, will probably,* and *will.* After the review, give the students time to use the modals in sentences that state the possibility of rain tomorrow. They should write a given sentence where they think it belongs on the modal thermometer. If you have an overhead projector, check the students' choices by covering all but one portion of the thermometer as you begin to go up the temperature gauge. Students like the suspense and the idea of the rising temperature. If necessary, explain the terms *Fahrenheit* and *Celsius* to the students and discuss the probable temperature range of the modals listed on the thermometer. While this "thermometer" provides students with a visual breakdown of modals of possibility, other activities and extended lessons in this chapter allow for more contextualized practice of these modals.

5.4. Modals of Advice: *Could, Should, Ought to, Had Better, Must,* and *Have To*

> **Visual focus/Research; L, S, W; i & iiiii**
> **Materials included**

The modal thermometer in Appendix 5.4a helps students distinguish between modals of suggestion, advice, and necessity: *could, should, ought to, had better, must,* and *have to.*

You can make the presentation of this list more interactive by giving students a work sheet with the modals left off (see Appendix 5.4b for a copy of this handout). Review the modals of advice. Then tell the students that you have a toothache and ask them what you should do. Have them write their advice using the appropriate modals in ascending order on the thermometer gauge. Again, if possible, check the students' responses using the overhead projector. Cover up each portion of the thermometer until you are ready to refer to that section. Students like the suspense and the idea of the rising temperature. If necessary, explain the terms *Fahrenheit* and *Celsius* to the students and discuss the probable temperature range of the modals listed on the thermometer.

 Take this opportunity to point out that *should* is also a rather strong form of advice and that the students should be aware that native speakers of English don't always use *should* or other modals when asking for or giving advice in person. Introduce your students to other expressions that are used when giving advice. For example, when someone asks for advice about a toothache, a person may respond without using modals at all as in

- Try + *ing*   Try rinsing your mouth with warm
                                      water.
- What/How about . . . ?   What/How about going to the dentist?
- Have you tried . . . ?   Have you tried taking medicine?
- Have you thought about . . . ?   Have you thought about going to
                                      the dentist?
- Why don't you . . . ?   Why don't you go to the dentist?

And sometimes people use *maybe* or *might* to soften their advice.

- You might try going to a dentist.
- Maybe you should talk to a dentist about it.

possibility / adverb

 Also, although the imperative form is generally thought of as being used to command someone to do something, people sometimes use this form as a means of leaving off *you should*. So, instead of giving a person with a toothache advice such as, "You should buy some pain medicine," a person might say, "Buy some pain medicine." Although the imperative form is used, students should not necessarily interpret this as an authoritative command but rather as helpful advice. In this situation, much depends on the intonation used.

Finally, people sometimes give advice by simply relating their own experiences without using modals or other expressions at all. Again in the case of a toothache, someone might say:

- When I had a toothache, I went to the dentist right away.

If it's possible, have your students ask native speakers for advice and note down the responses they get. As a class, share any new forms of giving advice that the students have heard and decide where they should be placed on the modal thermometer.

5.5. Modals of Possibility and Advice

Personalization; L, S, W; i & iii+

To more fully contextualize the students' understanding of the degrees of possibility, have them write a short description of what they imagine themselves doing in twenty years using the increasing degrees of possibility shown on the modal thermometer. For example:

> I could be a writer.
> I might be a short story writer.
> Maybe I'll have children.
> I'll probably live overseas.
> I'll be a teacher.

Then, to broaden the context, students can write similar sentences about the towns or cities they are from—How will their hometowns change in twenty or fifty years? Moving outward, students can then write about their respective countries, finally ending with possible statements about the future of the entire world. Have the students discuss their conclusions in small groups and consider the following questions.

> Why do they think one possibility is more likely to happen than another? Are all the changes positive? If not, how can these changes be avoided? For example, if a student has written that the world will probably be polluted in twenty years, what can be done to avoid this?

If your students are familiar with using modals of advice, have them use modals during their discussion whenever possible. For example, what should someone do if she wants to be a computer engineer in the future? What should someone do if he doesn't want more freeways built in his hometown or city? What should be done to stop water pollution?

5.6. Modals of Advice and Possibility

> **Problem/Solution; R, W; i & ii & iii+ & iiiii**

Have each student look for a short magazine or newspaper article related to a controversial or problematic topic the solution to which will impact many people. Ask them to summarize their articles in five to ten sentences. They should include a description of the events and people involved, and they should state the problem discussed in the article. Then ask the students to write a few sentences using the increasing degrees of advice that they would give to solve the problem or to resolve the controversy.

To model this activity for the students, bring in a short summary of an article for a class discussion. For example, an article in the July 5 issue of the *Economist* (1997) tells about a controversy in Russia over the appointment of President Boris Yeltsin's daughter as an official adviser to her father. In the article, Yeltsin's daughter, Tatiana Dyachenko, says that she was given this position because people often saw her when they wanted to speak with her father. Some people argue that it is not right for the president to appoint family members to governmental positions.

Based on this summary, students might come up with the following advice and/or outcomes.

- Yeltsin could ask his daughter to quit.
- The Duma could vote against her appointment.
- Dyachenko should resign.
- Dyachenko should not give up her job.
- The courts should say that her appointment is illegal.
- Dyachenko ought to keep her job because her father trusts her.
- If Dyachenko is qualified, she should keep her new job.
- Dyachenko must give up her position now.
- President Yeltsin must defend his decision.

With the students, discuss which suggestions are weaker and which are more aggressive. What might people think about the appointment of Dyachenko? How might Yeltsin and Dyachenko react to these suggestions? Encourage the students to debate advice that they disagree with and to provide alternative and/or additional suggestions. As a class, you can also discuss the political and/or social implications of the advice given. Of course, this particular example may be unfamiliar to your students and outdated, so you may want to look for more relevant materials to introduce in class.

Once you're sure that the students comprehend the summary, have them discuss what they think the end result of the situation might be. For example, in the case of Dyachenko's appointment:

- She could resign.
- People might continue to complain about her appointment.
- She'll probably stay in her position.

It is then interesting to compare the students' predictions with what eventually happens. In this case, Dyachenko remained in her position.

Once you've modeled the activity, have pairs or small groups of students share their summaries of an article and discuss the possible advice and/or outcomes that could logically follow from the situation described in the article. For best results, give the students time at home to write their summaries. Check their work before they share it in groups.

5.7. Using Modals

> **Second identity/Visual focus; L, S; ii & iiiii**
> **Materials included**

Bring in some pictures that depict a humorous or an emotionally charged situation. Have the students decide what a person or persons in the picture might be thinking. Ask the students to include modals in some of their responses. For example, picture a ballerina who is dancing in a row with other ballerinas; on her nose sits a huge bee; her eyes are crossed and she is grimacing. What is she thinking?

She might be thinking that . . .

the bee will sting her.
she will have to get out of line.
she can't move.

You can adapt this activity by changing the scenario to what the person might be saying to him- or herself. For example, the ballerina might be saying to herself (using as many modals as possible), "Oh, no, the bee is going to sting me and I'll have to yell. Then everyone will notice me, and I'll get fired. I should stand still." Again, you may want to explain to your students that when the verb *to think* is used to mean to have an opinion, then it is used as a nonprogressive verb; however, when the verb describes a person's thoughts at a given moment, the progressive form *thinking* is used. You may also need to explain that people also use the expression *to say something to oneself* to express what a person's private thoughts happen to be. You can vary the format of this activity by having the students close their eyes and imagine themselves in the scene you describe. In either case, you may need to preteach some vocabulary before your students discuss the visual image.

You can have the students work in pairs to come up with ideas. Have them first describe their picture to the class and then tell the class what they think the person in the picture might be thinking or might be saying to himself or herself. The illustration of a birthday party found in Appendix 1.4 works well with this activity. The person whose birthday it is might be thinking, "I hope I can blow out all the candles" or "I hope my wish comes true." If you don't have any additional pictures that you feel are appropriate for this activity, simply ask your students to imagine a scene as you describe it orally. You may also want to point out that people often leave out the clause word *that* when they are speaking informally. This happens after verbs such as *think, know, hope,* and *believe,* and after adjectives as in *I'm happy, I'm glad, It's funny,* and *I'm surprised.*

You may want to point out to your students that people often use *should* when they are giving themselves advice but not necessarily when giving advice to someone else. So, a friend watching the birthday girl blowing out the candles might say to himself, "I should help her blow out all the candles" or "I shouldn't eat too much of this cake!" or "I should have bought her something else for a present." (You may need to introduce your students to the form of the modal *should + have + participle* used in the past.)

Introduce your students to the expression *There are too many shoulds in my life!* Ask the students what part of speech *should* takes in this sentence and why they think this is so. The students should notice that *should* is used as a plural noun in this expression. Additionally, you can point out that people also use *should* when they are not sure about what to do. (See activity 5.9 for an activity in which *should* is used to express indecision.)

You can also use this activity to practice degrees of possibility and giving advice by having the students use modals to describe what could, might, may, will probably, and/or will happen next to the character in the picture and what the character(s) in the picture could, should, ought to, have to, and/or must do. If you have done activity 5.1 with your students add *have to, get to,* and *need to,* to the list of modals.

5.8. Using Modals

> **Cartoons; L, S, W; i & iii+**
> **Materials included**

Blank out the words in a cartoon that are written in the speech balloons or draw in speech bubbles if the cartoon only includes a caption (see Appendix 1.5 for a sample cartoon). If you want to give your students more room to write, simply number each character and have the students write below the illustrated materials. Have the students make up their own words for the cartoon using modals that fit the scene(s) depicted in the cartoon. (It isn't necessary for the students to understand the original text of the cartoon although you may want to share the text with them if there is one.) Give the entire class the same cartoon to work on and see what variations the students come up with. If it's logistically possible, select a variety of cartoons and give a cartoon with three characters to three students to work on, a cartoon with four characters to four students, and so on, so that each person in your class is identified with one character in a given cartoon. When you are using more than one cartoon, it is helpful to project the cartoon being discussed using the overhead projector so that all the students can see the original version while their classmates are reading what they've written.

For a variation of this activity, you could simply ask the students to write out a given character's private thoughts. Again, the students should use modals in their writing. You may want to remind the students that people often use the modal *should* when they are giving advice to themselves.

 ## 5.9. Using *Should* to Express Indecision

> **Making choices; L, S; i & ii & iiii**
> **Materials included**

Explain to your students that people use *should* not only to give advice to themselves and others but also to express uncertainty when they are making a decision about something important. Ask your students if they are familiar with the expression *Should I stay or should I go?* which was popularized by the band the Clash in a song by the same name, "Should I Stay or Should I Go?" (© 1982 Wineden Limited). In this song, the speaker is trying to decide whether or not he should stay in a relationship with someone. It's fun to share a recorded version of the song with your students, but you needn't do so to complete this activity.

To give your students practice using *should* to express indecision, give them a copy of the situations found in Appendix 3.3 and ask them to re-phrase the situations using *should* so that the first example, *You are about to graduate from high school. You have the choice to go on to college or not,* could be rephrased as the question, "Should I go to college or not?" or "Should I go to college or work full time?" Have the students work together to rephrase the statements on the work sheet and then discuss the results as a class. You can also ask the students to write questions using *should* that relate to deci-sions they are in the process of making or will have to make in their own lives.

Extended Lessons

5.10. *Can* and *Could:* Personalization

5.10a. Presentation

> Question formation; L, S; ii & iiiii
> 5 minutes

Make three columns on the board. In the first column write the first-person form of the verb for three things that you *can* do; in the second column, write three things you *can't* do; and, in the third column, write three things you *could* do when you were younger but not now. If you feel your students are familiar with the use of *wish + could,* add a fourth column in which you list things you *wish you could* do.

cook Indian food	play soccer	run 5 miles	play the violin
teach English	teach math	do the splits	ski well
write songs	have a cat	play in the afternoon	have a cat

Read through the information on the board and discuss any new vocab-ulary items. Then ask the students to guess why you've written this informa-tion on the board. Together, give each column a heading from left to right.

1. Things I can do
2. Things I can't do
3. Things I could do when I was younger (but not now!)
4. Things I wish I could do

Once you've given each column a heading, have the students form questions to elicit the information found in each column. For example:

1. What can you do?
2. What can't you do?
3. What could you do when you were younger?
4. What do you wish you could do?

You can also have the students work in pairs asking one another about your abilities: What can she or he do? etc.

5.10b. Practice

> Personalization; L, S; ii
> 10 minutes

Have the students make columns that pertain to their own lives. In pairs they can practice asking one another about their abilities.

5.10c. Application

> Summarizing; W; i
> 15 minutes/Homework

After the students have had the opportunity to discuss their abilities, ask them to summarize the information from their charts by writing a paragraph about themselves.

5.10d. Review

> Error correction; R, W; i & ii & iiiii
> 10 minutes

Collect the students' writings and note down grammar errors related to the use of *can* and/or *could*. Type these up to make an error correction work sheet. When you type the sentences, correct any errors that are not directly related to the modals. Give each student a copy of the work sheet (or project a copy of the work sheet using an overhead projector) and have them work individually for a few minutes to find and correct the errors. Then they can check their answers in pairs or as a class. You may want to check half the sentences one day and check half the next as a warm-up activity (see Appendix 4.6d for a sample error correction work sheet related to the present perfect). For variation, you could also use information from the students' writing to make a "Find Someone Who" information gap activity using *can* and *would*. (Refer to extended lesson 4.6e for an explanation of such an activity.)

5.11. Giving Advice: Advice Columnist

5.11a. Presentation

> **Advice columnist; L, S; iiiii**
> **5 minutes**

To contextualize the idea of giving someone advice, you can bring in a letter written to a newspaper's advice columnist such as Dear Abby, who is popular in the United States. You may want to preteach the term *advice columnist* since some students may not be familiar with such a profession. Also, you may want to explain that while some advice columnists address personal concerns, others give advice about etiquette, while others give advice about household jobs. Abby gives people advice about problems in their lives. Point out that people usually write in anonymously to Abby and use pseudonyms to protect their identity. The pseudonym relates to the problem a person is writing Abby about or the way the person feels such as "Fed up in Canada," "Disappointed in Detroit," or "Sleepless in Seattle."

5.11b. Practice

> **Discourse analysis; L, S, R; i & ii & iiiii**
> **Materials included**
> **20 minutes**

Have the students read a Dear Abby letter. Follow the approach outlined for the reading of the Dear Abby letter found in this stage. Since the letter and Abby's response are copyrighted, you will need to project the copyrighted materials on a screen using an overhead projector or obtain permission from the copyright holder to make copies of the letter. (Questions to accompany the letter also can be found in Appendix 5.11b.)

As the students read the letter for the first time, ask them to write down the ways in which the person writing has asked for advice. (Or, if you have obtained permission to make copies of the letter, ask the students to underline the information.) In the model provided, the author asks, "What do I do in the meantime?" and "Should I insist they speak in English so I can understand them—or what?" The students might be interested to notice that the writer doesn't always use modals when asking for advice. Next, have the students assume the identity of the writer and summarize orally, in pairs, the writer's problem using the first-person point of view.

Then have the students look at the advice Abby has given. Ask the students to write down or underline any modals and imperatives she uses. As a class or in pairs, give the students the opportunity to discuss what they think about Abby's advice—how might they feel if the advice had been written to them?

The students will probably notice that Abby does not necessarily use modals. Sometimes she uses imperative forms, and sometimes she gives a possible solution. For example, in the model provided, instead of writing *You should ask Yuri to compromise,* Abby writes, *Ask Yuri to compromise.* And instead of writing *You should suggest that he ask his friends to speak English part of the time they spend with you,* Abby writes, *Suggest that he ask his friends to speak English part of the time they spend with you.* You can point out that even though Abby has used the imperative form, this form comes across as being less bossy and even friendlier than if she had used a series of *you should* or *you ought to* statements.

Also, the students should notice that instead of writing, *You should take a Russian class,* Abby tells her reader, *A crash course in Russian would be a good beginning in overcoming the language barrier.* Here Abby simply states a possible solution. Even though students will need to be familiar with modals for grammar exams, they should also be aware that, as shown in this letter to Dear Abby and in her response, native speakers of English don't always use modals when asking for or giving advice.

If you haven't done so already, take the opportunity to introduce your students to other forms that are used when giving advice such as

Try + *ing*	Try going to a Russian class.
• What/How about . . . ?	What/How about going to a Russian class?
• Have you tried . . . ?	Have you tried going to a Russian class?
• Have you thought about . . . ?	Have you thought about going to a Russian class?
• Why don't you try . . . ?	Why don't you try taking a Russian class?

You can add that people sometimes use *maybe* or *might* to soften their advice.

- You might try going to a Russian class.
- Maybe you should try going to a Russian class.

Finally, a person might simply give an example of what she or he did in a similar situation.

- I took an intensive Russian language course, and that really helped me.

5.11c. Application

As an application, you could have your students do one of the following options.

Option One

> **Letter writing; W; i & ii**
> **20 minutes/Homework**

For homework, have the students assume a second identity and write anonymous letters to an advice columnist by taking a name such as "Broken-hearted in Las Vegas" or "Tired to death in Los Angeles" just as people do when they write to an advice columnist in the newspaper. In class, or as homework, the students can exchange letters and respond to them as if they were Abby. In addition to using modals, encourage them to use some of the other forms for giving advice that you've introduced in class.

Option Two

> **Letter writing; W; i & iii+ & iiiii**
> **20 minutes/Homework**

Bring in one letter written to a Dear Abby column, or make your own, and, for homework, have each student write a response to the letter as if she or he were Abby. Again, encourage them to use some of the other forms for giving advice that you've introduced in class as well as modals. In class, have the students get in groups of three or four to share their responses and to decide which response gives the best advice. As a class, share the responses that have been chosen for the good advice they give.

5.12. Expressing Preferences: Song

5.12a. Presentation and Practice

> Preferences; L, S; ii & iiiii
> 10 minutes

As a preteaching exercise for the expression of preferences, ask the students to choose which they'd rather be or do from each of the following pairs.

> a sparrow or a snail
> a hammer or a nail
> a swan or a snake
> a forest or a street
> to feel the earth beneath your feet or to fly in an airplane

Discuss any vocabulary questions the students may have. Give the students a chance to share their preferences with a partner and to explain why they've made these choices. Then share the results as a class.

5.12b. Practice

> Cloze exercise; L, S; i & ii & iiiii
> 10–15 minutes

If you are unable to find a copy of the Simon and Garfunkel song "El Condor Pasa (If I Could)" (© 1972 Columbia Records), proceed to the application stage of this lesson. If you are able to find a copy of the song, make a cloze exercise using the song lyrics. Leave blanks for the structure(s) you would like your students to practice. You can write the cloze on the board or project it on a screen. Let the students read through the cloze before they listen to the lyrics. Ask them to predict what might go in the blanks and to discuss any new vocabulary. Then play a recording of the song, or, if you don't have access to a taped version, simply read the lyrics aloud. As the students listen to the lyrics for the first time, have them circle or write down the preferences expressed in the song. The second time they listen to the lyrics have them fill in the phrases that are missing from the cloze exercise. Because the song is so repetitive, students generally find it easy to complete the cloze.

Give students the opportunity to compare their answers in pairs. Then discuss the song lyrics as a class. Have the students practice reading the lyrics aloud, paying particular attention to the pronunciation of the contracted form of *I would.*

You might like to discuss what is meant in the song by *to sail away* and *to be tied up to the ground.* Additionally, you may need to explain that the expression *to feel the earth beneath one's feet* has a metaphorical meaning as well as a literal one. Metaphorically it can mean to have common sense as opposed to not having common sense, i.e., *living with one's head in the clouds.*

5.12c. Application

Whether or not you were able to share the song lyrics with your students, you can have them complete Option One in the application stage of this lesson. To complete Option Two, students will need to be familiar with the song lyrics.

Option One

> **Drawing; L, S; i & iiiii**
> **20–30 minutes/Homework**

Have the students come up with their own list of things they'd rather be. If you have time, let the students make drawings of the things they'd rather be or have them cut out pictures from a magazine or calendar to complete their sentences. For example, a student might draw the following.

I'd rather be a   than a   .

Then the students can share their drawings with the class. Let the students try to guess how to complete the sentence. Give them time to ask the student why, in this case, she or he would rather be a butterfly than a cat. Encourage the students to come up with a number of comparisons and explanations.

Option Two

> **Songwriting; W; i & iiiii**
> **20–30 minutes/Homework**

Give the students the opportunity to write their own "If I Could" song. Suggest that they try to choose words that fit the rhythm of the original version. Before the students write their own version of the song, you may want to have the class examine what the images in the song have in common and what ideas unify them, for example:

- The speaker wants to fly away or get away from his usual life (the sparrow and the swan reflect this desire).
- The speaker also wants to be in control of what's going on in his life (the image of the hammer and the expression *feet on the ground* suggest control).

Suggest that the students use images that share common themes and communicate an understanding of their personalities.

Appendix 5.2. *Must* and *Must Not*

A teacher talking to his or her young students about the rules of behavior in the classroom

A football coach talking to his or her team

A doctor talking to his or her patient who has a dangerous heart condition

A dentist talking to a patient who needs to take better care of his or her teeth and gums

A parent talking to his or her five-year-old child who is going out to play in the snow

An employer talking to an employee who has been late for work too often

A police officer talking to a person who has just been arrested for car theft

A lawyer talking to a client about his or her upcoming court case

Appendix 5.3a. Modal Thermometer—Possibility

"Will it rain tomorrow?"

100% Fact

99% Certainty

90% Likely

50–75% Strong possibility

Less than 50% Weak possibility

No modals = It is raining!

It will rain tomorrow.

It will probably rain tomorrow.

It may rain tomorrow.
Maybe it will rain tomorrow.
It might rain tomorrow.
It could rain tomorrow.

Appendix 5.3b. Modal Thermometer—Possibility

Name(s)_____

"Will it rain tomorrow?"

100% Fact   No modals =

99% Certainty

90% Likely

50–75% Strong possibility

Less than 50% Weak possibility

Appendix 5.4a. Modal Thermometer—Giving Advice

"I have a toothache. What should I do?"

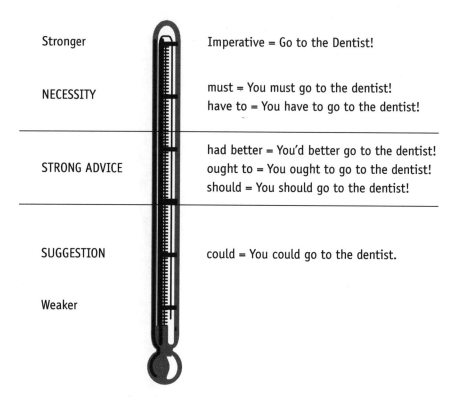

Stronger — Imperative = Go to the Dentist!

NECESSITY
must = You must go to the dentist!
have to = You have to go to the dentist!

STRONG ADVICE
had better = You'd better go to the dentist!
ought to = You ought to go to the dentist!
should = You should go to the dentist!

SUGGESTION
could = You could go to the dentist.

Weaker

Appendix 5.4b. Modal Thermometer—Giving Advice

Name(s)_____

"I have a toothache. What should I do?"

Stronger

NECESSITY

STRONG ADVICE

SUGGESTION

Weaker

Imperative =

-

-

-

-

-

© 1999 University of Michigan

Appendix 5.11b. Dear Abby: Modal Exercise

Letter to Abby

DEAR ABBY
Non-Russian-Speaking wife feels she's left out

ABIGAIL VAN BUREN
Syndicated columnist

DEAR ABBY: My husband, "Yuri," came here from Russia six years ago. We have been married five years. Yuri speaks excellent English. He has mentioned to me several times that it would be a good idea for me to learn Russian, but with two small children under 4, learning Russian has not been a high priority for me.

The problem is that Yuri has many Russian friends, mostly professional people who speak English very well. But when they come to visit, they speak in Russian, and I am left out.

Last Sunday, "Natasha" came over. I served cookies and coffee and tried to be a good hostess. She directed all her conversation to Yuri. When I asked her about her children and her job, she gave me brief answers in English, then turned to Yuri and continued speaking to him in Russian.

I realize she's Yuri's friend. I'm not jealous of her, nor do I suspect they are having an affair. I just think it's very rude of her to ignore me when she's here.

Abby, it's not just Natasha. It has gotten to the point that when his Russian friends come over, I go to our bedroom and watch TV. It's the same when we go to Natasha's house — or Sergei's or Ilona's. Their husbands and wives all speak Russian, and I'm left to play with the children. When I tell Yuri how I feel, he says it is much easier for them to express themselves in Russian than in English.

I have decided to learn more Russian, but what do I do in the meantime? Should I insist they speak in English so I can understand them — or what?

—Fed up in Canada

Abby's Response

DEAR FED UP: Ask Yuri to compromise; suggest that he ask his friends to speak English part of the time they spend with you, while you learn their language. A crash course in Russian would be a good beginning in overcoming the language barrier. Also, ask Yuri to teach you a few phrases every day. You'll be amazed at how quickly you can join in their conversations.

Letter to an Advice Columnist

Name(s)_____

Part One

Read the letter to Dear Abby. As you read, note down the ways in which the author asks for advice and any modals that are used in the letter.

    A.   The ways people have asked for advice

    B.   Modals that are used in the letter

Letter to an Advice Columnist

Name(s)_____

Part Two

1. In your own words, write what the writer's problem is and what advice she wants.

2. How has the author signed her name?

3. Read Abby's response. Does she use any modals in her response? Which ones? Why do you think she uses so many imperatives?

Chapter 6
Gerunds and Infinitives

Itemized Reference List

Skill Areas		Group Work	
Listening	L	Individual	i
Speaking	S	Pair	ii
Reading	R	Small Group	iii+
Writing	W	Class	iiiii

Structure		Activity	Skills	Groups	Appendix
Supplementary Activities					
6.1.	Gerunds and Infinitives	Riddle	L, S, W	i & iii+	
6.2.	Infinitives	Lists	L, S	i & ii & iiiii	177
6.3.	Infinitives	Quotation	W	i & ii & iiiii	
6.4.	Gerunds	Signs/ Personalization	L, S	i & iiiii	
6.5.	Infinitives and Gerunds	Sentence completion	L, S, W	ii & iiiii	
6.6.	Infinitives	St. Francis of Assisi	L, S, W	i & ii & iiiii	
Extended Lessons					
6.7.	Infinitives of Purpose: Professions				
6.7a.	Presentation	Professions	L, S	iiiii	
6.7b.	Practice	Professions	L, S, W	i & iii+	178
6.7c.	Application	Making conclusions	L, S, W	i & iii+ & iiiii	
6.8.	Infinitives: Ecclesiastes				
6.8a.	Presentation	Questions	L, S, W	i & iii+ & iiiii	179
6.8b.	Practice	Cloze	L, S	i & ii & iiiii	180
6.8c.	Application	Personalization	W	i	

Supplementary Activities

6.1. Gerunds and Infinitives

> Riddle; L, S, W; i & iii+

Explain that in Greek mythology the Sphinx is described as a creature with the head of a woman and the body of a lion. The Sphinx would kill and eat anyone who could not solve one of its riddles. In ancient Egypt, the Sphinx had the head of a man and the body of a lion. Tell the students that you are going to present the riddle of the Sphinx. See if they can guess what the riddle describes. (You might mention that the students don't have to worry about being eaten if they can't solve the riddle!)

The Riddle of the Sphinx

- What crawls on all fours in the morning, walks on two legs in the afternoon, and walks on three legs in the evening?

- The answer is a human being in his or her lifetime: a person crawls as a baby, walks in his or her youth, and uses a cane in old age.

Then ask the students to consider what activities a person does in each phase of his or her life as it is divided by the Sphinx. In their descriptions, have the students use verbs that are commonly followed by gerunds and/or infinitives such as the following (you can brainstorm this list with your students).

to want
to decide
to continue
to hate
to think
to enjoy
to start
to love
to stop

For example, for the first stage described by the Sphinx, a student might write: *A baby wants to eat all the time. A baby starts to crawl at about six months. Babies love to be held,* etc.

The idea is to describe the three major stages in life using verbs that are followed by gerunds and/or infinitives. Ask the students to write three to five sentences for each stage: for a baby, a youth, and an older person. Then they can share their work in groups of three or more. Your students may want to add additional stages to the three given by the Sphinx. If your students have completed activity 1.7, you can have them refer to the materials they have already provided for additional ideas.

6.2. Infinitives

> **Lists; L, S; i & ii & iiiii**
> **Materials included**

People in the United States are known for writing lists to themselves as a reminder of what they need to do during the day. Such a list might read:

buy stamps
mail letters
meet Steve for lunch
clean my room
call Mom

Have the students guess why you have written this list on the board. Explain that this list represents things you need, plan, expect, want, or hope to do as well as things you have to do or get to do. Point out that you are using infinitives to express your future plans. Based on the given list, the students might conclude that you need to buy stamps, you have to mail some letters, you plan to or get to meet Steve for lunch, you have to clean your room, and you need to call your mom. This is a good time to draw the students' attention to the inferential meanings that can be made on the basis of the infinitive which is used. For example, if you were to say, "I need to call my mom," one could infer that there might be some urgent reason for the phone call whereas if you were to say, "I plan to call my mom," one could infer that the phone call is nothing out of the ordinary. (See activity 5.1 for a further discussion of *have to, get to,* and *need to.* If you'd like, you could also have your students use the modal *should* to express a future necessity.)

Once the students have discussed your list, ask each student to make a list of at least four things she or he intends to do the following day. In pairs, the students should read over each other's lists and then ask appropriate questions such as "What do you have to do tomorrow?" "What do you plan to do in the afternoon?" "What do you need to do tomorrow?" etc.

While the students are discussing their own lists, write up the following list that pertains to the life of Ernest Hemingway. (Or, if your students are not familiar with Hemingway's life, create a list for a person with whom your students are already acquainted.)

She or he _____

> go fishing.
> meet Scott Fitzgerald for drinks.
> spend time writing *For Whom the Bell Tolls*.
> watch a bullfight.

First, have the students work orally to create sentences about this person's plans for the following day, i.e., "She or he plans to go fishing." "She or he gets to meet Scott Fitzgerald for drinks." "She or he needs to spend time writing *For Whom the Bell Tolls*." "She or he wants to watch a bullfight." See if the students can guess whose list it is. You will find sample lists in Appendix 6.2. The solution to the lists found in Appendix 6.2 is as follows.

1. The President of the United States
2. Marilyn Monroe
3. William Shakespeare
4. Margaret Thatcher
5. The Princess of Wales
6. Paul McCartney

If your students are not familiar with the people listed in the materials provided, you may need to make new lists for people with whom your students are more familiar. In this activity, I have used the present tense for the lists which pertain to people who are no longer living, but you may want to have your students use the past tense in such cases. Once the students have practiced the activity, you can also have them make lists which pertain to people from their own countries.

6.3. Infinitives

> **Quotation; W; i & ii & iiiii**

In Shakespeare's play *Hamlet,* the main character for whom the play is named, says the famous line "To be or not to be? That is the question" (3.1.55). You can point out to the students that this line is particularly easy to remember because of the parallel structure used with the infinitive forms. (For a discussion of parallelism, see extended lesson 1.11.) And, at the same time, a simple form is used to express a profound thought. Ask the students to discuss in pairs what Hamlet meant by the question, "To be or not to be?" Then, as a class, discuss the students' opinions. After the students are comfortable with the form and meaning of the quote, let them experiment with their own "To be or not to be" sentences. Tell them that they should also write a brief explanation of what the question suggests. For example, a student might write, *To laugh or not to laugh? That is the question,* and then give an explanation such as "Sometimes it is hard to laugh at yourself, but it is important to have a sense of humor."

6.4. Gerunds

> **Signs/Personalization; L, S; i & iiiii**

In the United States, there are many signs that tell people what they can or can't do in a given place. Signs that signal that an activity is not permitted in a particular place generally show a simple picture with a diagonal line running through the drawing. Draw the following sign up on the board and ask the students to tell you what they think it means using a gerund in their response.

(No smoking)

With the students, brainstorm other signs that show that a certain activity is not allowed, for example, no fishing, no camping, no swimming, no parking, etc. If you have time, you may want to discuss why such actions are often forbidden.

Then ask the students to come up with signs that represent something that relates personally to their dislikes and/or concerns and/or to things they can't do. For example, a student who is a vegetarian might draw a sign that symbolizes *no eating of meat.* A student who is concerned about air pollution might make a sign that symbolizes *no polluting of the environment,* and a student who can't ski might make a sign that symbolizes *no skiing.* Remind the students that their signs should express a progressive verb. Ask the students to make their own signs and draw them on the board or on a large piece of paper; then, as a class, the other students can try to determine the signs' meanings. You may want to caution the students not to make signs that might offend some of their classmates.

6.5. Infinitives and Gerunds

> Sentence completion; L, S, W; ii & iiiii

As a playful way to practice gerunds and infinitives, share the following line with the students—"I forgot to remember to forget him or her"—and ask the students what the speaker might mean. You can explain to the students that the line is being said by someone who wants to forget a relationship she or he had in the past but that this person is unable to do so. Ask the students to finish the sentence "I forgot to remember to forget . . ." with an experience they had in the past that they might like to forget but can't. Students generally pick up on the ironic use of the contradictory infinitives following one another, but you may want to emphasize the irony such an expression communicates so that students don't complete the sentence with memories of truly horrible experiences. Explain that they should focus on more lighthearted material and not on a personal tragedy. For example, a student might say, "I can't seem to remember to forget going on a blind date with someone I didn't like." You can point out that the sentence can be completed using a gerund or noun phrase. You may want to give the students the opportunity to write out their sentences and an explanation of what happened before sharing their experiences. Also, it's fun to have the students ask one another, "What can't you remember to forget?"

6.6. Infinitives

> **St. Francis of Assisi: L, S, W; i & ii & iiii**

To have students practice using infinitives, introduce them to a portion of the St. Francis of Assisi prayer. St. Francis (1182–1226) was born and lived in Central Italy. He is known for having given up his wealth and possessions to live a life of poverty. He started the Holy Order of the Franciscans, who took vows to live in poverty and to help the poor. Centuries later, Mother Teresa (1910–97), a Catholic nun who received a Nobel Peace Prize in 1979 for her ministry among the poorest of the poor in India, had those who worked with her say St. Francis's prayer daily. Once you have given your students this background information, write the following verbs on the board.

> to console
> to love
> to understand

Discuss any vocabulary questions. Then add the following items on the board and ask the students the difference between the sets of verbs.

> to console   to be consoled
> to love   to be loved
> to understand   to be understood

The students should notice that the verbs in the second group have been changed into the passive form and that someone is receiving the action of the verb rather than doing it for someone else. Once the students understand the difference between the two forms, share this part of the prayer with them by writing it up on the board, on flip chart paper, on an overhead transparency, or by dictating it to the students.

> [G]rant that I may never seek so much to be consoled as to console, to be understood as to understand, to be loved as to love with all my soul.

Let the students read the excerpt in pairs and discuss its meaning. Then discuss the students' ideas as a class.

At this point, have the students add other verbs that work thematically both in the infinitive and passive forms such as the following.

to help	to be helped
to give	to be given
to guide	to be guided
to counsel	to be counseled
to listen	to be listened to
to encourage	to be encouraged
to advise	to be advised
to forgive	to be forgiven

After the class discussion, have the students write a paragraph about one or more of the pairs of verbs. For example, a student could write about a time they gave someone a special gift and a time they were given a meaningful present.

Extended Lessons

6.7. Infinitives of Purpose: Professions

6.7a. Presentation

> Professions; L, S; iiiii
> 10 minutes

Tell the students that you are going to read some sentences about a profession using the first-person point of view. The students should imagine that you are actually someone else with a different profession. From these sentences, the students should be able to guess what "your" job probably is. (Please note that you may want to change the profession referred to in the presentation stage so that it focuses on a profession that is culturally relevant to your students.) Ask the students to listen for the infinitives as you read.

a. I clean the animals' cages every day *to give* the animals a healthy environment.
b. I feed the animals food every day *to keep* them healthy.
c. *To breed* in a zoo, the animals must feel safe and comfortable.

Given these sentences, the students might guess that they are being said by someone who works at a zoo, a zookeeper, and/or a veterinarian. To check the students' understanding of the causal relationship in the sentences and the use of the infinitive form, ask the following questions and direct the students to use an infinitive in their answers.

a. Why do I clean the cages every day?
b. To keep the animals healthy, what do I do?
c. How must animals feel to breed in a zoo?

You can point out to students that they can also use the structure *in order to* to express these relationships.

a. I clean the animals' cages every day *in order to give* the animals a healthy environment.
b. I feed the animals food every day *in order to keep* them healthy.
c. *In order to breed* in a zoo, the animals must feel safe and comfortable.

You may want to explain that the use of *in order to* sounds formal and that the use of the infinitive phrase without *in order to* sounds more informal or natural. Be sure to draw the students' attention to the fact that infinitive phrases can be used to begin a sentence.

6.7b. Practice

> Professions; L, S, W; i & iii+
> Materials included
> 10 minutes

With the students, generate a list of professions. Students should then choose a profession from the list and write three sentences from the first-person point of view using an infinitive phrase. Then, in groups of three or more, have students read what they've written for a profession and have the other students guess what kind of job the person has. Since this structure can be difficult for students, you may want to collect their work and check it before the students do the group work. If you think your students will have difficulty generating example sentences, you can give them the list in Appendix 6.7b and have them guess what profession is represented by the information provided in a given list. The professions listed in this activity are common to industrialized societies. You may need to adapt the materials if you think your students will not be familiar with some of the professions referred to in the activity.

The professions described in Appendix 6.7b are as follows.

1. a firefighter
2. the vice president of a company, a business consultant, or a manager
3. an English teacher
4. a doctor
5. a chemist

6.7c. Application

> Making conclusions; L, S, W; i & iii+ & iiiii
> 20 minutes

After the students have discussed the various professions, have them make conclusions a professional might make using the following structure: *It is + adjective + for (someone or something) + infinitive.* For example, the zookeeper presented in 6.7a might say:

It is necessary for us to preserve animal species.
It is important for animals to live in healthy conditions.
It isn't right to mistreat animals.
It is impossible for humanity to live without wildlife.

Take the time to model this activity before the students try it on their own. You may want to give the students time to write out their ideas before they share them with their classmates in small groups and/or as a class.

6.8. Infinitives: Ecclesiastes

6.8a. Presentation

> Questions; L, S, W; i & iii+ & iiiii
> Materials included
> 15 minutes/Homework

In preparation for a passage from the book of Ecclesiastes, one of the thirty-nine books of the Jewish Bible, write the following set of questions on the board or project them on a screen using an overhead projector.

1. A. When is it a good/bad time to plant crops?
    B. When is it a good/bad time to harvest crops?

As a class, come up with answers to these questions. The students will most likely answer the questions literally, but you can also point out that the questions have a metaphoric meaning because *to plant crops* can also refer to the efforts a person makes to develop skills and *to harvest a crop* can refer to receiving the benefits of one's labors. Once you've discussed the possible answers to these two questions, have the students work in pairs or small groups to discuss their responses to the additional sets of questions found in Appendix 6.8a. Then discuss their responses as a class. To save time and to give the students the opportunity to develop more thoughtful responses to the questions on the work sheet, you can have them write out their responses to the questions as homework. They can then discuss their answers in small groups and as a class the following day. Be sure, however, to discuss the first set of questions in class before the homework is assigned. Whether the questions are answered in oral or in written form, you may want to forewarn the students that some of the questions are controversial and deal with emotionally charged topics. Instructors should note that the sets of questions deal with some of the most difficult topics found in the excerpted passage. However, not all of the topics found in the passage are discussed in the presentation stage.

6.8b. Practice

> Cloze; L, S; i & ii & iiiii
> Materials included
> 10–15 minutes

Explain to the students that the source of these questions is Ecclesiastes, a book from the Jewish Bible that is traditionally believed to have been written by King Solomon, one of the kings of ancient Israel. He reigned from 961 to 922 B.C. Whether or not Solomon wrote the text, the original author(s) used the poetic form of parallelism to express thoughts about life and death. (For more on parallelism, see extended lesson 1.11.)

Ask the students to listen to a reading of the passage and to fill in the blanks in the cloze exercise provided in Appendix 6.8b. Refer to the first page of Appendix 6.8b for the completed version of the cloze. (*Note:* These materials may be photocopied only if the copyright information is included on the copies.) Read through the passage twice and give the students time to check their answers in pairs before discussing the cloze exercise as a class.

Because this passage from Ecclesiastes is so lyrical, it has been used as the basis for the popular song "Turn, Turn, Turn" by a group from the United States called the Byrds (1965). If possible, bring in a recording of the song and play it for the students. Or, you could choose to simply read the lyrics to your students. Ask them to determine the ways in which the song differs from the original version of the passage. Here are a few differences.

- The song includes the chorus, which adds the words *turn, turn, turn.*
- The song changes the orders of some of the events so that the more positive actions come first and the more negative second.
- The song doesn't include all the verses that are found in Ecclesiastes.
- Instead of saying, "A time to love and a time to hate," the song uses the expression "A time of love, a time of hate."
- The author of the text has included the word *and* between opposing infinitive phrases, but in the song lyrics the word *and* is left out.

6.8c. Application

> **Personalization; W; i**
> **15 minutes/Homework**

Once you have discussed the passage (and possibly the song lyrics) with the students, ask them to relate their own lives to the verses from Ecclesiastes— was there a time in their lives for love? A time of hate? Their responses to these verses may be very personal, so it is a good idea to tell the students that their writings will be kept private.

You can also ask students to relate the verses in the passage to important times in the history of their own countries. When was there a time of national mourning or rejoicing? When was there a time of peace? A time of war? When was there a time to gain? A time to lose? Before students write about their own countries, you may want to focus on the history of a predominantly English-speaking country as a model for this activity. For example, the people of the United States experienced a time of national mourning in response to the assassination of Dr. Martin Luther King, Jr., in 1968. A time of national rejoicing took place when Apollo 11 landed on the moon in 1969.

Appendix 6.2. Lists

---

1. She or he _____

- set up a meeting with the foreign minister of Russia
- meet with the vice president at 12:00
- play golf
- get ready for a White House dinner

---

2. She or he _____

- meet Arthur for lunch
- sign autographs
- go to photo shoot at 3:00
- study script for *Some Like It Hot*

---

3. She or he _____

- visit the Globe Theater
- finish writing *Macbeth*
- buy some more ink
- meet players in a London pub

---

4. She or he _____

- meet with Helmut Kohl at 11:00 for tea
- meet with the House of Lords at 1:00
- work on a chapter of *The Downing Street Years*
- write a speech on privatization

---

5. She or he _____

- visit the children's hospital
- attend a charity fund raiser
- buy a dress for an upcoming ball
- call the Queen Mother

---

6. She or he _____

- talk to Ringo
- check tour schedule
- answer fan mail
- finish writing "Let It Be"

Appendix 6.7b. Professions

1. a. To protect myself from smoke, I wear a mask.
   b. In order to save people's lives, I sometimes have to go into burning buildings.
   c. I use a fire extinguisher to put out fires.

2. a. To help a company run more smoothly, I make decisions about how to manage the company's money.
   b. I supervise departments to make sure that they are working well.
   c. I report to my boss to let her know how the company is doing.

3. a. I prepare lessons to help my students improve their English.
   b. To prepare my students for exams, I give them homework.
   c. I give my students opportunities to speak in class in order to make them more confident when speaking English.

4. a. I prescribe medicine to people to help them get well.
   b. I give people advice in order to help them avoid getting sick.
   c. When people feel sick, they come to me in order to get help.

5. a. To do my work, I need a special laboratory.
   b. I do experiments in order to discover new chemicals.
   c. I have to wear special protective clothing to protect my skin from dangerous chemicals.

Appendix 6.8a. Questions

1. A. When is it a good/bad time to plant crops?
   B. When is it a good/bad time to harvest a crop?

2. A. When is it a good/bad time to dance?
   B. When is it necessary/not necessary to mourn?

3. A. When is it a good/bad time to laugh?
   B. When is it a good/bad time to weep?

4. A. What does it mean to embrace an idea?
   B. What does it mean to refrain from embracing an idea?

5. A. What does it mean to gather stones?
   B. What does it mean to throw away stones?

6. A. What does it mean to sew something?
   B. What does it mean to tear something?

7. A. Is there ever a good time for war?
   B. Is there ever a time when killing is accepted?

Appendix 6.8b. Ecclesiastes 3:1–8

Complete Version

For everything there is a season,
And a time to every purpose under heaven:
a time to be born, and a time to die;
a time to plant, and a time to harvest;
a time to kill, and a time to heal;
a time to break down, and a time to build up;
a time to weep, and a time to laugh;
a time to mourn, and a time to dance;
a time to throw away stones, and a time to gather stones together;
a time to embrace, and a time to refrain from embracing;
a time to seek, and a time to lose;
a time to keep, and a time to throw away;
a time to tear, and a time to sew;
a time to keep silence, and a time to speak;
a time to love, and a time to hate;
a time for war, and a time for peace.

Appendix 6.8b. Ecclesiastes 3:1–8: Cloze

Name(s) _____

For everything there is a season,

And a time to every purpose under heaven:

a time _____, and a time to die;

a time to plant, and a time _____;

a time _____, and a time to heal;

a time to break down and a time _____;

a time _____, and a time to laugh;

a time to mourn, and a time _____;

a time _____ stones, and a time to gather stones together;

a time _____, and a time to refrain from embracing;

a time to win, and a time _____;

a time _____, and a time to throw away;

a time _____, and a time to sew;

a time to keep silence, and a time _____;

a time_____, and a time to hate;

a time for war, and a time for peace.

Chapter 7

Conditionals: Using *If* to Express Unreal Past Situations and Using *Wish*

Itemized Reference List

Skill Areas		Group Work	
Listening	L	Individual	i
Speaking	S	Pair	ii
Reading	R	Small Group	iii+
Writing	W	Class	iiiii

Structure		Activity	Skills	Groups	Appendix
Supplementary Activities					
7.1.	Using *Wish*	Personalization	L, S	ii & iiiii	
7.2.	Using *Wish*	Second identity	L, S, W	i & iii+	194
7.3.	Using *If*: Unreal Situations in the Past	Technology	L, S, W	iii+ & iiiii	
7.4.	Using *If*: Unreal Situations in the Past	Historical time line	L, S, R, W	i & iii+	195
7.5.	Using *If*: Unreal Situations in the Past	Dr. Seuss	R, W	i & ii & iiiii	199
Extended Lessons					
7.6	Using *Wish* and Unreal Situations in the Past: Dr. Martin Luther King, Jr.				
7.6a.	Presentation	Making wishes	L, S	iii+ & iiiii	
7.6b.	Practice	Sentence transformation	L, S, W	iii+ & iiiii	
7.6c.	Application	Second identity	W	i	200
7.7.	Using *If Only:* Song				
7.7a.	Presentation	Movie theme song	W	i & ii & iiiii	
7.7b.	Practice	Sentence completion	L, S, W	iii+ & iiiii	201
7.7c.	Application	Personalization	W	i	

Supplementary Activities

7.1. Using *Wish*

> Personalization; L, S; ii & iiiii

As a way to personalize the use of *wish*, ask the students what kinds of things people from different countries do when making a wish for good luck. Write these up on the board. You may come up with a list such as the following.

- Rubbing old teapots for good luck
- Crossing the first and second fingers
- Blowing out a candle on a birthday cake
- Throwing coins into a fountain or pond
- Touching something old

You can point out that in the United States it is common to make a wish upon a star. Then share the following children's rhyme with the students.

> Star light, star bright,
> I wish I may,
> I wish I might,
> Have the wish
> I wish tonight . . .
>
> (Followed by a silent wish)

Ask the students to repeat the lines to practice their rhythm. You can have the class read the lines chorally with sections of the class alternating each line. Then ask the students to make their own wish to complete the poem. Explain that the wish doesn't have to be personally revealing but can be something general such as "I wish I could visit Paris" or "I wish I could meet Michael Jackson," etc. Suggest that the students make more than one wish. In pairs, they can repeat the rhyme and, at the end of it, share their wishes. You can then ask individual students in the class to ask one another about their wishes.

If a student mentions that wishes don't come true if they are told to other people, you can say that is generally thought to be the case except for in ESL classes!

As a follow-up exercise, ask the students to discuss what they would do if their wishes were to come true. For example, one student might ask his or her partner, "If you could go to Paris, what would you do?" and the partner might respond by saying, "If I could go to Paris, I would visit the Louvre. I would go out to French restaurants. I would practice my French, and I would go to cafés." You may want to encourage the students to practice the contraction *I'd* when they share their responses.

7.2. Using *Wish*

> **Second identity; L, S, W; i & iii+**
> **Materials included**

For this activity, you should refer to the lives of well-known people—living or dead—with whom your students are already familiar so that the students are not distracted by unfamiliar vocabulary when they practice making wishes. Explain to the students that you are going to read three wishes that a particular well-known person might have made when still a youth, before she or he became famous. To model this activity, you will need to have introduced your students to the life of Dr. Martin Luther King, Jr. (See activity 2.2 and extended lesson 3.11 for ways to present King's life to your students.) Read the following three wishes to the class and ask them to guess who might have made such wishes in their lifetime.

1. I wish I could work to end segregation.
2. I wish that I could give a speech called "I Have a Dream."
3. I wish that I had the power to convince people that racism is wrong.

After you have modeled the exercise, give each student a slip of paper with the name of a famous person written on it. Again, be sure to use the names of people with whom your students are familiar. Arrange it so that two or three students have the same person. Give the students time to respond in writing to the following prompt that you can write up on the board.

Imagine that you are _____ and that you are only fifteen. Write three wishes that you would like to come true in your lifetime.

If you would like, suggest that your students use specific verb forms in their responses such as *could, had,* and *were.*

After the class has had time to write out their responses, have the students who have written wishes for the same person get into groups to share what they've written. Then have each group select three of their wishes to present to the class. Ask the other students to guess which famous person is making the wishes.

To save class time, you can have the students make up the wishes on their own or use the ready-made wishes found in Appendix 7.2 as the basis for this activity. The people referred to in these materials are well-known figures from Europe and the United States. You may want to create a similar list of wishes for people with whom your students are more familiar. The Answer Key for the work sheet found in Appendix 7.2 is as follows.

1. Abraham Lincoln (1809–65)
2. Wolfgang Amadeus Mozart (1756–91)
3. Elizabeth Taylor (1932–)
4. Michael Jordan (1963–)
5. Vincent van Gogh (1853–90)
6. Robert Frost (1874–1963)

You can find an extended version of this activity in extended lesson 7.6.

7.3. Using *If:* Unreal Situations in the Past

> **Technology; L, S, W; iii+ & iiiii**
> **Materials included**

As a warm-up for this activity, you may want to go through activity 3.4 with your students, although this is not a requirement. Explain that you are going to describe what life would be like in industrialized societies if certain inventions and/or technologies had not been discovered. From your description, students should try to guess what the discovery was. For example, of the computer, you could say, "If this item hadn't been invented, global communication wouldn't be possible. The Internet would not have been created. We couldn't do office work as fast."

With the students, brainstorm a list of inventions and technological developments that have significantly impacted modern life. Ask each student to choose one item to write about or give each student an item from the list found in Appendix 3.4. Remind the students that they need to use *if* to express an unreal situation in the past since they are writing about what life would be like if the invention or technology had not been discovered. Then, as a class or in groups of three or more, ask each student to read out his or her clues while the others try to guess what invention or technology is being described. Please note that while I have used the expression *unreal situation in the past* to describe this form, you may choose to use other terminology with your students.

7.4. Using *If:* Unreal Situations in the Past

> **Historical time line; L, S, R, W; i & iii+**
> **Materials included**

In this activity, students will discuss what would have happened if a historical event had not occurred. To model this activity, give the students a copy of the historical time line found in Appendix 7.4a or project it on the overhead. Then give small groups of students the opportunity to read the information to one another and to discuss the meaning of the italicized terms and any other vocabulary terms they may not understand.

Once you feel the students are comfortable with the information and the vocabulary terms found in the time line, ask them to work individually to complete sentences A, B, C, and D from the handout in Appendix 7.4a, by referring to the information in the text. When the students have finished, have them share their answers in small groups.

Give small groups of students a copy of one of the historical time lines found in Appendixes 7.4b and 7.4c. First ask them to read the time line together and to look up new vocabulary words. Use this opportunity to go around the room to answer any questions the students might have. Then ask them to complete the sentences found on the handout working individually or as a group. Encourage the students to write additional sentences to accompany a given reading.

If time allows, have the students make similar time lines for homework and use these for additional practice exercises. Remind the students to use the present tense in their time lines.

7.5. Using *If:* Unreal Situations in the Past

Dr. Seuss; R, W; i & ii & iiiii
Materials included

Ask the students if they have ever heard of Dr. Seuss. If they have not, explain that Dr. Seuss is the pen name for an American writer of children's books, Theodor Seuss Geisel (1904–91) and that Dr. Seuss books are famous for their whimsical rhymes, nonsense words, and wacky artwork that Seuss created himself. One book that Seuss wrote is called *Happy Birthday to You!* and, as the students might imagine, the book describes the events on a child's birthday. This book is narrated by the Birthday Bird, who wonders what it would have been like if the birthday boy in the story had never been born. Before you begin the activity, ask the students to share associations they have with birthdays in the United States such as cakes, candles, presents, etc.

Put the passage from Appendix 7.5 on the board, on an overhead transparency, or on a piece of flip chart paper. If you have time, you could choose to dictate the passage to your students. If you choose to dictate the passage, it's fun to pause just before the rhyming words *do, tree, tomatoes, doesn't,* and *pleasant* to let the students guess what the rhyming words are. Before you present the passage, you may want to preteach words such as *toad, doorknob,* and *baked potatoes*—words that are not usually associated with birthdays! Give the students time to read the text silently to themselves. After that, have them read it to one another in pairs, alternating lines from the passage. Take a few minutes to discuss any vocabulary questions as a class. Ask the students to identify where the verb *wasn't* is used as a noun instead of a verb as in "Why you might be a WASN'T!" Have your students discuss the meaning of *a wasn't.*

This passage lends itself to intonation practice, so it's fun to model the intonation for the students one line at a time and then have them repeat each line after you. Encourage the students to practice the intonation related to the questions and the exclamations and the added stress given to the capitalized words. Point out that the last line should be read as an exclamation, not a question. Once the students have had the chance to practice the intonation in pairs, have them read the passage chorally.

When the students are comfortable with the excerpt's content, draw their attention to the question, "If you'd never been born, well then what would you do?" Point out that a person couldn't actually do much if they'd never been born, so you are going to have them think about what they wouldn't have done if they'd never been born. Model a few sentences using examples from your own life such as

1. If I hadn't been born, I never would have fallen in love.
2. If I hadn't been born, I wouldn't have visited the Grand Canyon.
3. If I hadn't been born, I never would have eaten chocolate.

Have the students write out their sentences and then share them in pairs and/or as a class. Some of the example sentences may seem a bit silly, but they allow for a fun and nonthreatening way to personalize and to practice a grammatical structure that students often find difficult.

To make this activity more thought provoking, you can then have the students write out sentences about how other people's lives would have been different if they'd never been born or had never done certain things and how the past actions of others have affected your students' lives.

1. If my mother hadn't met my father, I never would have been born.
2. If I hadn't been born, my mother (or father) wouldn't have had a daughter (or son).
3. If my brother hadn't been born, I would have been an only child.

You can then have the students expand their focus to include historical figures and events such as

1. If Hitler hadn't invaded other European countries, World War II might not have started.
2. If Martin Luther King, Jr., hadn't been born, the Civil Rights Movement in America might not have taken place.

Extended Lessons

7.6. Using *Wish* and Unreal Situations in the Past: Dr. Martin Luther King, Jr.

7.6a. Presentation

> **Making wishes; L, S; iii+ & iiiii**
> **10–50 minutes**

To complete this lesson, your students will need to be familiar with the life of Dr. Martin Luther King, Jr. If your students are not familiar with King's life, you may want to take two days to complete this lesson. To introduce your students to the events in King's life, complete the extended lesson presented in 3.11. You can also use the outline found in Appendix 2.2 for further information about King's life.

Once your students are familiar with King's life and legacy, complete activity 7.2 to prepare them for the practice stage of this lesson. As in activity 7.2, ask the students to imagine that Dr. Martin Luther King, Jr., is only fifteen years old and that they are going to share three wishes he might have made at that age before he became well known. You can model the following wishes for the students.

1. I wish that all races could live together in peace.
2. I wish I could end segregation.
3. I wish that I could give a speech in front of the Lincoln Memorial in Washington, DC.

Ask the students to write some additional wishes that King might have made. If you would like, suggest that your students use specific verb forms in their responses such as *could, had,* and *were.* Have the students get into small groups to share their wishes.

7.6b. Practice

Sentence transformation; L, S, W; iii+ & iiiii
15 minutes

Once the students have shared their additional wishes, have them transform the three original wishes by writing why Dr. King would have wanted the three previously stated wishes to come true. For example, King might have said:

1. If all races could live in peace, people would have equal chances.
2. If I could end segregation, racial conflict would end.
3. If I could give a speech in front of the Lincoln Memorial in Washington, DC, I could convince thousands of people that racism is wrong.

Ask the students to write similar statements for any additional wishes they may have written in the presentation stage. Have the students discuss these situations in their small groups and then as a class.

You can then ask the groups of students to make inferences about the world at the time the wishes were made based on the information found in the *if* clause sentences. For example:

1. People didn't have equal chances.
2. Racial conflict had not ended.
3. Many people thought racism was not wrong.

As a follow-up activity to this stage, ask the students whether or not all of King's "wishes" came true.

7.6c. Application

> Second identity; W; i
> Materials included
> 15+ minutes/Homework

Ask students to think of another well-known person and write three wishes that this person might have made as a fifteen year old. However, be sure to have the students select people who have previously been discussed in class so that they won't have to deal with unfamiliar vocabulary to complete this portion of the lesson. Then repeat the stages presented in the practice portion of this lesson: (1) Have the students write out why this person would want these wishes to come true, (2) Ask the students to write out the inferences that can be made on the basis of these wishes. To help the students organize their sentences, you may want to have them use the outline in Appendix 7.6c.

7.7. Using *If Only:* Song

7.7a. Presentation

> Movie theme song; W; i & ii & iiiii
> 15 minutes

To present a context for the practice of *if only,* write the title *The Wizard of Oz* on the board and ask if any students are familiar with this movie. If some students do know the story, ask them to name some of the characters in it and discuss the story's plot. If students aren't familiar with the movie, explain that it is a popular American film (© 1939 MGM) based on the book *The Wonderful Wizard of Oz* written in 1900 by L. Frank Baum. In this movie, Dorothy, a girl who lives in the state of Kansas, is caught up in a cyclone that takes her to a magical land called Oz. During Dorothy's adventures in Oz, three characters help her: the Tin Man, who is like a tin robot that chops wood, the Cowardly Lion, who is always afraid, and the Scarecrow, who usually stands in a cornfield to scare away birds. Each character in the story needs something in particular: while Dorothy needs to find a way to get back home to Kansas, the Tin Man needs a heart, the Lion needs courage, or nerve, and the Scarecrow needs a brain. (You may want to point out that the article *the* is used with *nerve* to make an abstract or uncountable noun more concrete and more emphatic. This can also be done with nouns such as *time, crime, truth, life,* and *law:* i.e., if I only had the time, I would help; the crime in this city is terrible; this is the life; the law is there to serve you.)

Ask your students to imagine how the following statements might be completed by the characters in *The Wizard of Oz.*

Dorothy: If I only had a way to get home, I_____

_____

The Tin Man: If I only had a heart, I _____

_____

The Lion: If I only had the nerve, I _____

_____

The Scarecrow: If I only had a brain, I_____

_____

In pairs, have the students share their completed sentences and then discuss these as a class. Check to see that the students have used the correct form to complete the sentences.

7.7b. Practice

> Sentence completion; L, S, W; iii+ & iiiii
> Materials included
> 15 minutes

Put the students in groups of four or more and assign one of the characters to each group so that they can make an extended list for their character. So, for example, the group writing about the Scarecrow might write:

If I only had a brain, . . .

> I would be a genius.
> I would win a Nobel Prize.
> I wouldn't be wrong all the time.
> I would be good at math.

Point out that the order of the sentences can be reversed.

I would win a Nobel Prize . . .
I wouldn't be wrong all the time . . .
I would be good at math . . .

> if I only had a brain.

Once the groups have prepared their sentences, they can read them out to the class with each person sharing what she or he has written.

Then introduce the song entitled "If I Only Had a Brain (If I Only Had a Heart) (If I Only Had the Nerve)" from the movie *The Wizard of Oz*. Portions of the lines sung by each character can be found in Appendix 7.7b. Project the lyrics using an overhead transparency or write them up on the board or on flip chart paper and have the students read the lyrics and decide which character is singing. The key to the lyrics is

1. the scarecrow,
2. the tin man,
3. the lion.

Once the lyrics have been assigned to the proper characters, you can put the students into groups of three and have them take on the roles of the Lion, the Scarecrow, and the Tin Man respectively. Before the students read through the song on their own, you may want to explain some of the word-plays or puns in the lyrics—these are noted on the work sheet found in Appendix 7.7b. These wordplays add to the charm of the lyrics. While some students may feel that such language is not useful, you can point out that people often use wordplays in social situations and it is indeed helpful to be aware of this rhetorical device. You may also want to preteach some of the vocabulary found in the lyrics such as

to unravel a riddle
tender
sentimental
to deny something (idiomatic: There's no denying it.)
fate

If you're able to get a copy of the film on video, watching it makes for a fun extracurricular class activity. (However, please note that permission is required to show a film in class.) Your students might be interested to know that at the end of the story the Scarecrow realizes he is clever; the Tin Man feels that he has a heart; the Lion discovers that he has courage; and Dorothy finds out how to get back to Kansas—she need only click the heels of her ruby shoes and repeat, "There's no place like home."

7.7c. Application

> **Personalization; W; i**
> **10–15 minutes/Homework**

Have the students write verses for a personalized version of the "If I Only . . ." song. If you have access to the tune, students can try to write lines to accompany the music. They might choose concrete objects or abstract ideas as prompts: "If I only had a car . . . ," or "If I only had a million dollars . . . ," or "If I only had the time. . . ."

Appendix 7.2. Wishes

1. A. I wish that I could be the sixteenth President of the United States.
    B. I wish that I could end slavery in the United States.
    C. I wish that people would build a memorial in my honor.

    My name is _____

2. A. I wish that I could write over six hundred musical works.
    B. I wish that I could write operas.
    C. I wish that I could be remembered as a famous composer of the eighteenth century.

    My name is _____

3. A. I wish that I could grow up to be a famous actress.
    B. I wish that I could win two Academy Awards.
    C. I wish that I could marry Richard Burton.

    My name is _____

4. A. I wish that I were a famous basketball player.
    B. I wish that I could score over three thousand points in a single basketball season.
    C. I wish that I could play for the Chicago Bulls.

    My name is _____

5. A. I wish that I were a well-known Dutch painter.
    B. I wish that my paintings sold for millions of dollars.
    C. I wish that I could paint the perfect sunflower.

    My name is _____

6. A. I wish that I were a famous American poet.
    B. I wish that I could write a poem for President Kennedy's inauguration.
    C. I wish that I could write a poem about fire and ice.

    My name is _____

Appendix 7.4a. Historical Time Line

Name(s) _____

Use information from the reading to complete the sentences found below.

Heliocentric Theory

1543 Nicolaus Copernicus, a Polish *astronomer, theorizes* that the earth and other planets *orbit* around the sun and that the earth does not stay in one place as believed. His theory is called the *heliocentric theory*—or sun-centered theory—but he cannot prove his theory because the telescope has not yet been invented.

1608 Hans Lippershey, a Dutch *spectacle* maker, develops the form for the *telescope.*

1609 Galileo, an Italian astronomer, uses Lippershey's ideas to make his own telescope. Using the telescope, he proves Copernicus's heliocentric theory is correct by following the movements of the *planet* Venus. Galileo supports Copernicus's theory.

A. If the telescope had already been invented, Copernicus _____

_____

B. If Galileo had not proved Copernicus's theory, people _____

_____

C. If _____, Galileo would
not have seen Venus.

D. If _____, he would not
have seen Venus.

E. _____

_____

F. _____

_____

Appendix 7.4b. Historical Time Line

Name(s)_____

Use information from the reading to complete the sentences found below. Then add a few sentences of your own.

The Discovery of DNA's Shape

1951 Maurice Wilkins studies the structure of the deoxyribonucleic acid (DNA) *molecule,* a nucleic acid involved in carrying *genetic traits* from one *generation* to another. DNA is thought to be the basic element of all living things. Wilkins's use of *X rays* helps him to *hypothesize*—or make an educated guess—that the DNA molecule has a double-*spiral* structure.

1953 Using research developed by Wilkins, James Watson and Francis Crick *construct* a model of the DNA molecule.

1956 Arthur Kornberg chemically produces a DNA molecule, thus proving experimentally the double-spiral structure of a DNA molecule theorized by Watson and Crick.

1959 For his experiment in DNA, Kornberg receives a *Nobel Prize.*

1962 Wilkins, Watson, and Crick receive the Nobel Prize for their work.

1. If Maurice Wilkins had not guessed that the DNA molecule has a
    double-spiral structure, then _____

    _____

2. If Watson and Crick had not used Wilkins's research, _____

    _____

3. If _____ ,
    Kornberg wouldn't have received a Nobel Prize.

4. If _____ ,
    Watson and Crick wouldn't have won the Nobel Prize.

5. _____

    _____

6. _____

    _____

Appendix 7.4c. Historical Time Line

Name(s)_____

Use information from the reading to complete the sentences found below. Then add a few sentences of your own.

The Development of the English Language (a very short time line!)

449–1066 Old English: A west *Germanic* language spoken by the Angles, Saxons, and Jutes who invaded Britain in the fifth century. They borrowed some words from the early Britons or Celts whom they had conquered. Two of these words are believed to be *cart* and *down*. About 140 words from *Latin* such as *mass, priest, kitchen,* and *pear* were brought into Old English during this period. About 40 words were brought into Old English by the *Vikings: cut, ugly, both,* and *ill* are among these words.

1066–1450 Middle English: The French (who were then called the Normans) invade England, and, as a result, French words such as *nobility, royal,* and *regal* are introduced into English.

1450–1660 Modern English Period: Borrowing from other languages becomes even more common. During the *Renaissance,* many words from Latin such as *agile* and *catastrophe* are introduced into English. And Shakespeare himself borrows from the Latin to create such words as *accommodation, assassination,* and *obscene.* Words from over fifty languages enter the English language during this period.

Twentieth-Century English: Over 750 million people speak English. Because many words from foreign languages have been *incorporated* into English, the number of words in English is quite large: the *Oxford English Dictionary* lists 500,000 words in the English language whereas German dictionaries typically have 185,000 words and the French vocabulary has 100,000.

1. Words like *cut* and *ugly* might not have entered the English language if

    _____.

2. If the French had not invaded England, _____

    _____.

3. If Shakespeare hadn't borrowed from Latin, _____

    _____.

4. The *Oxford English Dictionary* wouldn't list so many words if _____

_____.

5. _____

_____

6. _____

_____

Information from *The Story of English* by R. McCrum, W. Cron, and R. MacNeil (New York: Viking Press, 1986). Exercise © 1999 University of Michigan

Appendix 7.5. Dr. Seuss

If we didn't have birthdays, you wouldn't be you.
If you'd never been born, well then what would you do?
If you'd never been born, well then what would you be?
You *might* be a fish! Or a toad in a tree!
You might be a doorknob! Or three baked potatoes!
You might be a bag full of hard green tomatoes!
Or worse than all that . . . Why, you might be a WASN'T!
A Wasn't has no fun at all. No, he doesn't.
A Wasn't just isn't. He just isn't present.
But you . . . You ARE YOU! And, now isn't that pleasant!

Appendix 7.6c. Wishes   Name(s) _____

A. Write three wishes a famous person might have made at the age of fifteen.
    1.

    2.

    3.

B. Write the reasons this person would want each of the wishes to come true.
    1.

    2.

    3.

C. Write the inferences you can make based on each of the previous three reasons.
    1.

    2.

    3.

Appendix 7.7b. Song

E.Y. Harburg

IF I ONLY HAD A BRAIN (IF I ONLY HAD A HEART) (IF I ONLY HAD THE NERVE)

1. I'd unravel every riddle for any **individle**
   in trouble or in pain.
   With the thoughts I'd be thinkin'
   I could be another **Lincoln**
   if I only had a brain.

2. I'd be tender, I'd be gentle, and awful sentimental
   regarding love and art.
   I'd be friends with **the sparrow**
   and **the boy that shoots the arrows**
   if I only had a heart.

3. I'm afraid there's no denyin'
   I'm just **a dandy-lion,**
   a fate I don't deserve.
   But I could show my **prowess,**
   be a lion, not **a mowess,**
   if I only had **the nerve.**

---

individle: individual (Here it is misspelled to rhyme with *riddle*.)
Lincoln: Abraham Lincoln, the sixteenth American president. He is famous for ending slavery in America.
the sparrow: a small bird. Here *the* functions to show that the speaker would be friends with sparrows in general and not just one specific sparrow.
the boy that shoots the arrows: Cupid, the god of love. He is often shown as a small baby with wings who shoots magic arrows at a person's heart to make him or her fall in love with someone.
a dandy-lion: a play on the word *dandelion,* a weed with a yellow flower. *Dandy* is also an adjective meaning *fine, good,* as in *He is a good lion.*
prowess: strength and power
a mowess: a wordplay on *a mouse.* A mouse is considered to be weak and fearful. Also, *mowess* rhymes with *prowess.*
to have the nerve to do something: to be brave enough to do something

Chapter 8
Connecting Words

Itemized Reference List

Skill Areas		Group Work	
Listening	L	Individual	i
Speaking	S	Pair	ii
Reading	R	Small Group	iii+
Writing	W	Class	iiiii

Structure	Activity	Skills	Groups	Appendix
Supplementary Activities				
8.1. *Either/Neither* Pronunciation	Song	L, S	i & ii & iiiii	220
8.2. Using *Either/Or*	Role play/Register	L, S, W	ii & iiiii	222
8.3. Using *Neither/Nor*	Parallelism	L, S, W	i & ii & iii+ & iiiii	
8.4. Connecting Ideas	Making deductions	L, S, R, W	i & ii & iii+	
8.5. Using *And*	Poem	L, S, R	i & ii & iiiii	223
8.6. Using Connectors	Dictation and drawing	L, S, W	i & ii	
8.7. Using Connectors	Sentence completion	R, W	i & ii & iiiii	224
Extended Lessons				
8.8. Using *Because:* Poem				
8.8a. Presentation	Word association	L, S	i & ii & iiiii	
8.8b. Practice	Discourse analysis	L, S, R	ii & iiiii	225
8.8c. Application	Poem	W	i	
8.9. Using Connectors				
8.9a. Presentation: Option One, Part One	Sentence completion	L, S	iiiii	226
8.9a. Presentation: Option Two, Part One	Matching	L, S	i & iiiii	227
8.9a. Presentation: Option Two, Part Two	Analysis	L, S, R	iiiii	228
8.9b. Practice and Application	Logical story sequence	L, S, R, W	i & ii & iii+ & iiiii	229

Supplementary Activities

8.1. *Either/Neither* Pronunciation

> **Song; L, S; i & ii & iiiii**
> **Materials included**

Students often have questions about the differences between the pronunciations of some English words in the United States and in England such as the American and British pronunciations of *either* and *neither*. For a bit of fun, use George Gershwin's song "Let's Call the Whole Thing Off" to present some of the pronunciation differences between British and American English. In this duet, a conversation takes place between an American man and a British woman; they are thinking about calling off, or ending, their relationship because they can't agree on how to pronounce certain words. However, in the end, they decide to stay together and to "call the calling off off." It's interesting to note that Gershwin was American and his wife was British. To introduce the song, write the title on the board and have the students guess what the song is about based on the title. You can then tell them about the background information related to the song.

Project the words to the song onto a screen using an overhead projector (see Appendix 8.1 for a copy of the lyrics). Explain that the words in the song are sometimes spelled as they should be pronounced. However, the spellings are written as found in the original song lyrics and not according to a standard phonetic alphabet. Also, ask the students to note down any new vocabulary words they find as they read through the song. Discuss the new vocabulary terms and then give the students time to work in pairs to experiment with the British and American pronunciations of the words *either, neither, potato, tomato, pajamas, laughter, after, vanilla, sarsaparilla,* and *oysters*.

Once the students have familiarized themselves with the lyrics, play a recording of the song, if possible. If not, read through the song for the students. As you go through the song, write up the pronunciations common to the United States and Great Britain. Again, remind the students that you are using the spellings used in the original song lyrics and not phonetic symbols. As a class, determine how the underlined portion of the words listed below should be pronounced. Then write the correct spelling of each word as shown.

United States	*Britain*	*Spelling*
<u>ee</u>ither	<u>eye</u>ther	either
n<u>ee</u>ither	n<u>ye</u>ther	neither
tom<u>a</u>to	to·m<u>ah</u>·to	tomato
pot<u>a</u>to	po·t<u>ah</u>·to	potato
pa<u>j</u>amas	pa·<u>jah</u>·mas	pajamas
<u>oy</u>sters	<u>er</u>sters	oysters
la<u>ug</u>hter	l<u>aw</u>fter	laughter
<u>a</u>fter	<u>aw</u>fter	after
van<u>i</u>lla	van<u>e</u>lla	vanilla
sa's'par<u>i</u>lla	sa's'par<u>e</u>lla	**sarsaparilla**

(You may want to point out that in the United States your students may hear both forms of pronunciation because of regional differences in pronunciation. You may also choose to have the students discuss the pronunciation of the words as they are listed before they actually listen to the lyrics.)

After you've clarified the pronunciation of the American and British forms, respectively, then have the class read through the song with half of the class using American pronunciation and the other half using British pronunciation while you narrate the main text.

If you don't have access to an overhead projector, write the first stanza of the song and the refrain on the board. Read through these with your students and discuss any new vocabulary words. Also, write up the British and American pronunciations of the words as they appear in the chart shown previously and have your students practice pronouncing the words in both columns. Ask the students to supply you with the actual spelling of each word and write this information up on the board as well. Once your students are comfortable with the pronunciation of the words found in the song, then read the text aloud to the class pointing to the appropriate word in a given column as it appears in the song and asking the students to say the word using the appropriate pronunciation. If you'd like, assign British pronunciation to one-half of the class and American pronunciation to the other. Ask all of the students to read the refrain together each time it appears in the song.

---

sa's'parella: (sarsaparilla) a sweet-flavored carbonated drink

8.2. Using *Either/Or*

> **Role play/Register; L, S, W; ii & iiiii**
> **Materials included**

Often, when students are introduced to the use of *either/or,* the structure is shown as a negative auxiliary as in *Sandy doesn't drink coffee and Pat doesn't either.* In general, students are rarely given an understanding of the social dynamics of an *either/or* proposition. To help students understand the social context of such a situation, model an *either/or* situation; for example, consider a conductor who is frustrated with the performance of a violinist. The dialogue between them might go as follows.

> *Conductor:* Either you have this piece memorized by tomorrow morning or I'll have another violinist take your place.
> *Violinist:* I'm sorry. Give me another chance. I'll be able to play the piece perfectly by tomorrow.
> *Conductor:* Well, we'll see what happens tomorrow. But, remember this, either shape up or ship out!

Act out the parts of the conductor and the musician for the students and have them guess what the situation is. After you've modeled a situation, have pairs of students write a dialogue that includes one or two *either/or* statements for one of the scenarios. (A ready-made list of *either/or* scenarios can be found in Appendix 8.2. However, you may want to make a list of scenarios that contains examples that are more relevant to your students' cultural context.)

As one pair of students acts out their scenario for the class, ask the other students to guess what the situation is. Once the scenarios have been presented, have the class discuss what characteristics the situations have in common. Elicit some of the following responses from the students.

- A person in authority is talking to someone who is under his or her authority.
- A person is talking to someone for whom she or he is responsible.
- The person making the *either/or* propositions wants the listener to change his or her behavior.
- It is not pleasant to be put in an *either/or* situation.
- It may be dangerous to put someone in an *either/or* situation because the person might not do what you asked, and then you'll have to follow through on your words.

8.3. Using *Neither/Nor*

> Parallelism; L, S, W; i & ii & iii+ & iiiii

Introduce the students to a well-known adage from Shakespeare's *Hamlet* (1.3.79). Polonius, a member of the king's court, tells his son, "Neither a borrower nor a lender be." Write the quote up on the board and give the students time to discuss in pairs why Polonius gave his son such advice. Then, as a class, discuss the students' opinions. Next, share Polonius's reasons with the class: "For loan oft loses both itself and friend/and borrowing dulls the edge of husbandry" (1.3.80–82). Explain that *husbandry* refers to a person's ability to manage his or her personal finances.

You can have the students try to come up with their own *neither/nor* advice using words or phrases. Have each student share his or her advice with the class explaining, as Polonius did, why the advice is sound. If you are pressed for time, have the students read their advice to one another in groups of three or more and then choose the best advice to share with the entire class.

8.4. Connecting Ideas

> Making deductions; L, S, R, W; i & ii & iii+

Have the students analyze situations from which they can deduce who might be responsible for a given situation using *either/or, neither/nor,* and/or *both/and.* Create a model for the students or use the examples given. Of course, the examples I have used to model the activity may be unfamiliar to your students and/or outdated, so you may want to look for examples that would be more relevant to your students. Topics related to politics, crime, and sports work well with this activity. For example:

1. The following is a summary of the article "Small and Not So Nameless" from the *Economist,* February 22–March 1, 1996, 33.

   In 1996, someone wrote a book called *Primary Colors,* a very true-to-life account of what went on inside Clinton's presidential race in 1992. The author of the book wrote it anonymously, but many people think that Joe Klein, a political columnist for *Newsweek,* wrote the book. He denied it, but a computer analysis of Klein's writing suggests that he did write the book.

Students might come up with the following statements based on this summary.

- Either Klein wrote the book or he didn't.
- Klein neither wrote the book nor does he know who did.

Here is another example.

2. In the 1990s, the trial of O. J. Simpson, an American football hero, captured the attention of many people in the United States. Simpson was accused of having murdered his wife. The following is a summary of the situation and of Simpson's explanation for his wife's death.

   Nicole Simpson, the wife of the American football hero O. J. Simpson, was found murdered in her apartment. Her husband, from whom she was getting divorced and with whom she was not living, claims that he was in his own home at the time of the murder and that she was murdered by members of a drug ring. The woman's family believes that the husband is responsible for the murder.

Students might make the following deductions.

- Either the husband is telling the truth or he is lying.
- Neither her husband nor members of a drug ring murdered her.
- Both the husband and the woman's family are mistaken about who committed the murder.

Since this activity may not be easy for intermediate level students, it might be helpful to have the students work in groups or pairs to complete this activity and/or to have the students work with summaries that you have already prepared rather than with summaries they have written themselves.

8.5. Using *And*

> **Poem; L, S, R; i & ii & iiiii**
> **Materials included**

Often, students think of the word *and* as simply combining two objects or ideas. They are generally not aware of the rhetorical effect the use of *and* can have, especially in writing. To illustrate the effects of *and* used repeatedly, look for poems such as "The Wind" by James Stephens (1882–1950) in which the author has used the word *and* for effect.

To introduce students to the topic presented in the poem "The Wind," ask them to brainstorm a list of terms that are used to refer to different kinds of wind. As students come up with ideas, list these on the board. Elicit the following terms from the students.

> a breeze
> a hurricane
> a typhoon
> a tornado

Then ask the students to think of adjectives that are associated with the wind such as the following.

> gentle
> soft
> breezy
> cool
> strong
> powerful
> wild
> angry
> destructive

It's also interesting to discuss how the wind manifests its presence and whether or not a person can actually see the wind.

Explain to the students that when a human emotion is given to something like the wind that is not human, then the writer has used the technique of personification. Ask pairs of students to read alternating lines of the poem paying close attention to the wind's personality. (For a copy of the poem, see Appendix 8.5.) Once the students have looked up new vocabulary words in their dictionaries, have them answer the following questions.

1. What is the wind's personality like? How can you tell?
2. What does the wind do to the leaves?
3. What does the wind do to the branches?
4. Can you think of situations in real life where people or societies have acted like the wind in the poem? (Because this question could elicit disturbing memories for some students, I would not press students for answers. If answers are not forthcoming, simply provide

examples such as World War I [1914–18], World War II [1939–45], and the dropping of the atomic bomb on Hiroshima [Aug. 6, 1945] and on Nagasaki [Aug. 9, 1945].)

Discuss the students' ideas about the wind as a class. The students should notice that the wind in this poem is violent and destructive and even obsessed with killing. Once the students are familiar with the content of the poem, ask them to go back and underline each time the poet has used the word *and.*

Have the students read the poem again, but this time in pairs, with one person reading the main text of the poem while the other person reads out only the word *and.* As the students read, ask them to notice how the poet has used the word *and* in the poem. Discuss the results as a class and elicit the following information from the students.

- In line 1, the poet uses *and* to connect the wind's first two actions.
- From line 2, until the end of the poem, the poet uses *and* to make one long sentence in which the actions of the wind take place, just like a steady gale of wind blowing.
- In lines 5 and 6, the poet uses *and* repetitively to emphasize the many killings that will take place. Also, the repetition of *and kill and kill and kill* suggests the repeated killings.

As the students can tell from this poem, the word *and* is not only used to combine words, phrases, and sentences but is also used for rhetorical effect. For a poem in which the use of *and* suggests enthusiasm and energy, see e. e. cummings's poem "in Just-".

8.6. Using Connectors: *Although, Even Though, If, Even If, Unless, While, Whereas,* and *Because*

> Dictation and drawing; L, S, W; i & ii

Please note that this activity should be used for practice only after you have already presented the connecting words *although, even though, if, even if, unless, while, whereas,* and *because* to your students. (For suggestions on how to present these words, see extended lesson 8.9.) In grammar textbooks, such words are referred to variously as subordinating adverbs, dependent clause words, and adverb clauses among other descriptors. For the purposes of this resource book, such words are simply categorized as connectors or connecting words; however, instructors should use the term that their students are accustomed to using.

For this activity, have the students place a piece of paper horizontally in front of them. Then tell them to draw a fairly large island in the middle foreground of the paper. On the island, they should then draw three stick figures: Timothy, Carlyn, and Joan. Next to these three figures, they should draw a large speech bubble.

Explain to the students that these three people have something in common: their ship has sunk and they're waiting for help on a deserted island. Give the students the opportunity to compare their drawings with one another to make sure that they have followed the directions correctly.

Once everyone has correctly drawn the scene, tell the students that you will dictate a series of sentences for which they should draw pictures to help them recall what you have said. They shouldn't try to write down the actual words. However, they may write down the connecting word that was used or they may prefer to draw a symbol for a word. Here you will find a copy of the dictation followed by a sample drawing of how this dictation might look when drawn.

Dictation

1. Although it was a large island, there was only one tree on it. A monkey was sitting in the tree.
2. Even though the sun was shining, Joan was wearing a coat.
3. Whereas Carlyn had a hat on, Timothy didn't.
4. Although a helicopter flew by, it was too far away to see them.
5. Even though a ship passed by, it went by without stopping.
6. Timothy was thinking that if they didn't get water soon, they would die.
7. Carlyn was thinking that unless they built a fire, no one would see them.
8. Timothy was fishing because he wanted to catch something to eat.
9. Joan was thinking that even if someone heard their call on the radio, it would be days before help arrived.
10. The monkey was wondering if the three people would ever leave the island.

Sample drawing

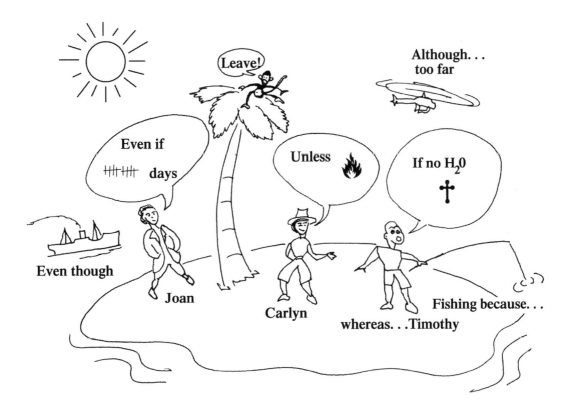

After the dictation, have the students try to recreate as many of the original sentences as they can based on their drawings. You can have the students write down the sentences they come up with and share them as a class. Encourage the students to write some additional sentences and dictate these to a partner or to the class so that they can be added to the drawing.

Although the scenario on the deserted island is rather unlikely and used primarily to get the students' attention, you can easily make up other situations that are more common and fairly easy to draw such as a rock concert, a dinner party, a wedding, or people fishing from a boat. Whichever situation you choose, make sure that your students are familiar with the vocabulary common to each situation before you begin the dictation.

Most likely, you'll find that some of your students are quite good at drawing and that they'd like to include fine details in their drawings, but, for the purposes of this activity, you'll need to encourage them to use simple stick figures and sketches. You may also want to point out that people rarely use such connectors one after another as in this activity. In this case, the intent is simply to help the students visualize the logic of a particular connector.

8.7. Using Connectors: *Although, Even Though, If, Even If, Unless, While, Whereas,* and *Because*

> Sentence completion; R, W; i & ii & iiiii
> Materials included

This activity helps students to understand the logical relationship between two sentences that are combined using *if, even if, although, even though, unless, while, whereas,* or *because.* This logical relationship is made clear through a series of five or more pairs of sentences that are related to a similar content. For example, the series of sentences used in this activity are about a baseball team called the Mariners from Seattle, Washington, in the United States.

For this activity, you will need to give your students the necessary background information they need to combine the sentences logically. Explain that the Mariners, a Seattle-based team, once had the chance to win a baseball championship. Their slogan was "Refuse to Lose." The Mariners didn't win the championship, but they played good baseball and made their fans happy. The Mariners also wanted the people of Seattle to support the building of a new stadium for their team, and they said they would move to another city if they didn't get a new stadium. Based on this information, the students should be able to logically combine each pair of sentences about the Mariners.

Be sure to tell the students that they can *only add connecting words; they may not change any of the other words* in the sentences. Additionally, they will need to change the punctuation to combine the sentences. You will find a handout of this activity in Appendix 8.7. Have the students discuss their changes in pairs and then as a class. The work sheet and the logical changes are as follows.

1. The Mariners refused to lose. They lost.
2. Many fans were happy. The Mariners won many games.
3. The Mariners didn't go to the finals. Everyone was still happy with their good performance during the year.
4. The Mariners get a new stadium. They will move to another city.
5. Many Seattle fans will be sad. The Mariners move.

Logical changes:

1. *Although* the Mariners refused to lose, they lost.
2. Many fans were happy *because* the Mariners won many games.
3. *Even though* the Mariners didn't go to the finals, everyone was still happy with their good performance during the year.
4. *Unless* the Mariners get a new stadium, they will move to another city.
5. Many Seattle fans will be sad *if* the Mariners move.

Since the topic of the Mariners is highly localized and dated, your students may not be interested in it, so it would be worthwhile to think of situations that are more relevant to them. If your students are familiar with a situation of global significance, such a topic would also work well. In either case, it is important to make sure that the students are familiar with the necessary background information so that they can make logical choices when choosing an appropriate connector.

Extended Lessons

8.8. Using *Because:* Poem

8.8a. Presentation

> **Word association; L, S; i & ii & iiii**
> **10 minutes**

As a creative way to practice the use of *because,* introduce the poem "I Shall Paint My Nails Red" by Carole Satyamurti (b. 1939). Before the students read the poem, ask them what adjectives, nouns, verbs, and adverbs they associate with the sentence "I shall paint my nails red." Discuss their associations as a class. Students may come up with the following associations.

    feminine
    danger
    passion
    carefully
    glamour
    sharp

(You may need to explain to your students exactly what it means to paint one's nails and introduce them to vocabulary such as *nail polish, enamel, nail polish remover,* and *manicure.*) Tell the students that these are some of the associations the poet has come up with.

    public service
    pride
    admire them in traffic jams
    survivor
    a ten-minute moratorium

Discuss any words that are new to the students. Then give them time to discuss in pairs and then as a class why the author of the poem might have made these associations. Also, have the students consider why the author has chosen to use *shall* rather than *will* in the title of the poem. You can point out that in British English, there is generally no difference in meaning between the two forms whereas in American English, the use of *shall* is considered to be more formal and emphatic. In British English, *will* is now used more often than *shall.* In American English, *shall* is rarely used.

8.8b. Practice

> **Discourse analysis; L, S, R; ii & iiii**
> **Materials included**
> **15–20 minutes**

Write the poem on the board or project it on a screen using an overhead projector (see Appendix 8.8b for a copy of the poem). Then give the students the opportunity to read the poem together in pairs, alternating lines. As the students read, ask them to think about why the author has chosen to repeat *because* so many times. Then read through the poem as a class, having a different student read each line.

Once the students have familiarized themselves with the poem, discuss why the author has chosen to begin each line of the poem with *because.* Among the possible responses, elicit the following response.

- There are ten reasons—one for each nail.

Discuss the last line of the poem with the students. What is meant by *reversible?* Why do they think the author has chosen this as the last line of the poem? Possible responses could be

- The woman has finished painting her nails and can easily take the polish off if she wants to.
- Unlike many situations in life, painting nails is something that can be reversed.

In pairs have the students discuss what they've learned about the speaker of the poem. Be sure to have the students give evidence from the poem to support their conclusions. This provides a good opportunity for students to review the use of *must* and *must not* to make a logical conclusion.

- She must live in an urban environment because she mentions cars, traffic jams, public service, etc.
- She considers herself a survivor, so she must have had some difficult situations in her life.
- She is or was married and has a daughter.
- She has a lover.
- She takes ten minutes to paint her nails.
- When the speaker paints her nails, she has ten minutes of peace.

8.8c. Application

> **Poem; W; i**
> **20+ minutes/Homework**

Have the students write a similar "I Shall . . ." poem, mimicking the author's style, based on something they will (or shall) do in the future.

"I will (or shall) buy a Porsche because . . ."
"I will (or shall) have children because . . ."

You may want to have the students write their poem as a homework assignment.

8.9. Using Connectors: *Although, Even Though, If, Even If, Unless, Whereas, While,* and *Because*

8.9a. Presentation

> **Matching; L, S; iiiii**
> **Materials included**
> **20–30 minutes**

Often students feel comfortable using *if, because,* and *while* to join dependent and independent clauses, but they are hesitant to use forms such as *even if, even though,* and *although.* This activity is meant to help students conceptualize the way these particular connecting words affect the logic of a sentence. The presentation stage of this lesson is meant only as a simplified introduction and so focuses on the present tense. It is also meant to appeal to learners who like to be given charts and outlines. Activities 8.6 and 8.7, as well as the practice and application stages of this lesson, provide students with activities that will help them to more fully conceptualize the information presented in this stage of the lesson.

To begin this presentation, give each student a slip of paper with either the dependent or independent clause of a sentence. You'll find a handout of ready-made slips in Appendix 8.9a, Option One, Part One (p. 226). Ask the students to stand up and find the person who has the other part of their sentences. Encourage the students to actually read their excerpts out loud to one another. After the students have found their partners, have each pair read their sentence to the class. To show that the clauses can move within the sentence, you can then have each pair switch places and read their sentence aloud again. Since there are only sixteen slips of paper, you may choose to use a matching activity to complete this portion of the lesson. You'll find a handout of a matching activity in Appendix 8.9a, Option Two, Part One (p. 227).

After having completed either Option One or Option Two, distribute copies of the original Appendix 8.9a Option One (p. 226) to your students. As a class, you will use this handout as the basis for a discussion of the logical meaning of the connecting words used in this lesson. To complete the handout, you will need to refer to the notes found in Appendix 8.9a, Part Two (p. 228). In this chart, the term *possible situation* is used to denote a situation that could possibly happen but hasn't yet, whereas the term *actual situation* denotes a situation that has actually happened or is true at the present moment (or will be true in the future). Sentences 1–4 describe possible situations whereas sentences 5–8 describe actual situations.

Ask your students to draw a line to separate sentences 1–4 from 5–8. Explain the term *possible situation* as it applies to the first four sentences and have the students conclude whether or not the action in the second portion of each sentence is expected or unexpected based on the given situation. After you've worked through the first half of the chart with your students, explain the term *actual situation* as it applies to the last four sentences and have the students conclude whether or not the action in the second portion of each sentence is expected or unexpected based on the given situation. In the end, the students should have added their own notes to the chart so that it looks like Appendix 8.9a, Part Two (p. 228). To save class time, you could simply give your students a copy of the completed work sheet and then discuss each sentence in turn.

Students are often confused by the meaning of *unless*. Although it is somewhat reductive, suggest that *unless* means *if not* only when *if not* means *except if.* Also, an *unless* clause can be followed by an affirmative result, i.e., *Unless it rains, he will go on holidays.* Finally, students should notice that the present tense is used with *unless* to express a future posisbility. You could also use this opportunity, or a future one, to point out that negative structures are not used in dependent clauses beginning with *unless* because the *un* in *unless* already suggests a negative, so to write a sentence such as *Unless it doesn't rain, he will go on holidays* would be similar to using a double negative and illogical.

While most students will be appreciative of the information and the chart you have discussed as a class, some may feel overwhelmed by all the input. Be sure to console such students by pointing out that they will now have the opportunity to apply this information in a creative way.

8.9b. Practice and Application

> Logical story sequence; L, S, R, W; i & ii & iii+ & iiiii
> Materials included
> 20–30 minutes/Homework

After you've introduced the use of *although, even though, if, even if, unless, whereas, while,* and *because,* then have the students apply their knowledge by making a set of illogical sentences logical by changing *only one word* in the sentence *without changing the connecting word used and without adding any words.* The group of sentences should be treated as a logical whole with the logic of a given sentence being dependent on the sentence(s) that precede it. The series of sentences used to model this activity is based on a marriage proposal. If your students are unfamiliar with the social custom of asking someone for his or her hand in marriage, you'll need to explain this custom to them. You will find a handout of this activity in Appendix 8.9b. As the students complete this activity, remind them to refer to the chart completed in the presentation stage. (However it is also possible to skip the presentation stage of this lesson if you think your students already have a thorough understanding of the connecting words used in this portion of the lesson.)

Before the students complete the work sheet individually or in various groups, do the first sentence together. Note that some students may write "Although Jean doesn't love Pat, she will marry him." While this sentence is grammatically correct, it is not in accordance with the directions that state "a word cannot be added to the sentence." Also, this sentence does not allow the rest of the story to develop logically. The sentence should read, "Although Jean loves Pat, she won't marry him." A possible solution to the activity is as follows.

1. *Although* Jean loves Pat, she <u>won't</u> marry him.
2. *Unless* Jean marries him, Pat <u>will</u> be single.
3. Pat <u>won't</u> buy a new tuxedo *because* he isn't getting married.
4. Pat still loves Jean *even though* she <u>won't</u> marry him.
5. *If* Jean decides to marry him someday, Pat will say "<u>yes</u>" because he still wants to marry her.

As a variation of this exercise, tell the students that they can change any word or words in the sentence they choose—except for the connecting word—without trying to keep a logical relationship between all five of the sentences. Collect the results and compile a list of the various choices students have come up with. For example, for the first sentence, students have made the following sentence.

1. Although Jean loves Pat, she will marry him.
    a. Although Jean doesn't love Pat, she will marry him.

and for the last sentence:

5. If Jean decides to marry him someday, Pat will say "no" because he still wants to marry her.
    a. If Jean decides to marry him someday, Pat will say "no" because he doesn't want to marry her anymore.
    b. If Jean decides to marry him someday, Pat won't say "no" because he still loves her.

It's interesting for students to see the way the connectors can change the meaning of a sentence, and it's important for students to have the opportunity to experiment with such forms.

Appendix 8.1. Pronunciation

George Gershwin

LET'S CALL THE WHOLE THING OFF

Things have come to **a pretty pass**—
Our romance is **growing flat,**
For you like this and the other,
While I go for this and that.
Goodness knows what the end will be;
Oh, I don't know where I'm at . . . .
It looks as if we two will never be one.
Something must be done.

You say eether and I say eyether,
You say neether and I say nyther;
Eether, eyether, neether, nyther—
Let's call the whole thing off!

Yes, you like potato and I like po-tah-to;
You like tomato and I like to-mah-to;
Potato, potahto, tomato, to-mah-to—
Let's call the whole thing off.

Refrain

But oh, if we call the whole thing off, then we must part.
And, oh, if we ever part, then that might break my heart.

So, if you like pajamas and I like pa-jah-mas,
I'll wear pajamas and give up pa-jah-mas.
For we know we
Need each other, so we
Better call the calling off off.
Let's call the whole thing off!

---

a pretty pass: a situation that has become difficult to deal with
growing flat: becoming uninteresting (like a soda drink without the carbonated bubbles)

Refrain

You say laughter and I say lawfter,
You say after and I say awfter;
Laughter, lawfter, after, awfter—
Let's call the whole thing off!

You like vanilla and I like vanella
You, sa's'parilla and I sa's'parella;
Vanilla, vanella, choc'late, strawb'ry—
Let's call the whole thing off!

Refrain

So, if you go for oysters and I go for ersters,
I'll order oysters and cancel the ersters.
For we know we
need each other, so we
Better call the calling off off.
Oh, let's call the whole thing off!

Appendix 8.2. Either/Or Situations

An angry parent talking to his or her son (or daughter) who has not passed a math exam in high school.

The manager of a company talking to his or her assistant manager who has arrived late to work three times in a row.

A soccer coach who is not happy with the way one of the team members performed during the last game.

A doctor who thinks that a patient will die of a heart attack if he or she does not follow the proper medical advice.

A dentist who thinks that a patient will soon lose his or her teeth to gum disease unless the patient follows the dentist's advice.

A police officer who has just stopped a driver for drunk driving.

A firefighter who has examined a factory and found many unsafe situations such as bad wiring and a lack of fire extinguishers. The firefighter is speaking to the factory owner about the problems he or she has found.

Appendix 8.5. Poem: Using *And*

James Stephens (1882–1950)

THE WIND (1915)

The wind stood up and gave a shout.	1
He whistled on his fingers and	
Kicked the withered leaves about	3
And thumped the branches with his hand	
And said he'd kill and kill and kill,	5
And so he will and so he will.	

Appendix 8.7. Connectors

Name(s) _____

Based on what you know about the Mariners, combine each pair of sentences logically. Add only *connecting words; do not change any of the other words* in the sentences. Also, you will need to change the punctuation to combine the sentences.

1. The Mariners refused to lose. They lost.

2. Many fans were happy. The Mariners won many games.

3. The Mariners didn't go to the finals. Everyone was still happy with their good performance during the year.

4. The Mariners get a new stadium. They will move to another city.

5. Many Seattle fans will be sad. The Mariners move.

Appendix 8.8b. Connectors

Carole Satyamurti (b. 1939)

I Shall Paint My Nails Red (1990)

because a bit of colour is a public service.
because I am proud of my hands.
because it will remind me I'm a woman.
because I will look like a survivor.
because I can admire them in traffic jams.
because my daughter will say ugh.
because my lover will be surprised.
because it is quicker than dyeing my hair.
because it is a ten-minute moratorium
because it is reversible.

Appendix 8.9a. Option One.
Part One: Sentence Completion

1. If she travels by train,

    it will only take her twelve hours to reach Moscow.

2. Even if John travels by air,

    he won't arrive in time for the meeting.

3. If John plans to travel,

    he'll need a passport.

4. Unless she gets a passport,

    she won't be allowed to travel in Russia.

5. Because she has money and time,

    she can afford to travel all over the world.

6. Even though her friend has money,

    she doesn't like to spend it on traveling.

7. She wants to travel in Russia

    whereas her friend wants to travel in China.

8. While she travels in Russia,

    her friend travels in China.

Appendix 8.9a. Option Two.
Part One: Matching

Name(s) _____

Match up the two columns to form complete sentences.

___ 1. If she travels by train,

a. she won't be allowed to travel in Russia.

___ 2. Even if John travels by air,

b. her friend travels in China.

___ 3. If John plans to travel,

c. she doesn't like to spend it on traveling.

___ 4. Unless she gets a passport,

___ 5. Because she has money and time,

d. it will only take her twelve hours to reach Moscow.

___ 6. Even though her friend has money

e. whereas her friend wants to travel in China.

___ 7. She wants to travel in Russia

___ 8. While she travels in Russia,

f. he'll need a passport.

g. she can afford to travel all over the world.

h. he won't arrive in time for the meeting.

Appendix 8.9a. Part Two: Analysis

1. If she travels by train, it will only take twelve hours to reach Moscow.
   Possible situation   Expected situation

2. Even if John travels by air, he won't arrive in time for the meeting.
   Possible situation   Unexpected situation

3. If John plans to travel, he'll need a passport.
   Possible situation   Expected situation

4. Unless she gets a passport, she won't be allowed to travel in Russia.
   Possible situation   Expected situation
   (If she doesn't get a passport . . .)
   (Except if . . .)

5. Because she has money and time, she can afford to travel all over the world.
   Actual situation   Expected situation

6. Even though her friend has money, she doesn't like to spend it on traveling.
   Actual situation   Unexpected situation

7. She wants to travel in Russia whereas her friend wants to travel in China.
   Actual situation   Unexpected situation
                               (in contrast to)

8. While she travels in Russia, her friend travels in China.
   Actual situation   Unexpected situation
                               (in contrast to or at the same time)

Appendix 8.9b. Connectors

Name(s) _____

Make each set of illogical sentences logical by changing *only one word* in the sentence *without changing the connecting word used*. Note that words cannot be added to the sentences. The group of sentences should be treated as a logical whole with the logic of a given sentence being dependent on its logical relationship to the other sentences.

1. *Although* Jean loves Pat, she will marry him.

2. *Unless* Jean marries him, Pat won't be single.

3. Pat will buy a new tuxedo *because* he isn't getting married.

4. Pat still loves Jean *even though* she will marry him.

5. *If* Jean decides to marry him someday, Pat will say "no" because he still wants to marry her.